T0134874

QoS Routing Algorithms for Wireless Sensor
Networks

K. R. Venugopal · Shiv Prakash T. ·
M. Kumaraswamy

QoS Routing Algorithms
for Wireless Sensor Networks

 Springer

K. R. Venugopal
Bangalore University
Bengaluru, India

Shiv Prakash T.
Vijaya Vittala Institute of Technology
Bengaluru, India

M. Kumaraswamy
Computer Science and Engineering
Sri Jayachamarajendra Polytechnic College
Bengaluru, Karnataka, India

ISBN 978-981-15-2722-7   ISBN 978-981-15-2720-3   (eBook)
https://doi.org/10.1007/978-981-15-2720-3

This Springer imprint is published by the registered company Springer Nature Singapore Pte Ltd.
The registered company address is: 152 Beach Road, #21-01/04 Gateway East, Singapore 189721, Singapore

Thyagaraj K
Rukmini T

Foreword

This book provides a systematic introduction to the fundamental concepts, major challenges, and effective solutions in Wireless Sensor Networking (WSN). Distinguished from other books, it focuses on the networking aspects of WSNs and covers the most important networking issues, including network architecture design, medium access control, routing and data dissemination, node clustering, node localization, query processing, data aggregation, transport and Quality of Service, time synchronization, and network security.

This book is a collection of state-of-the-art research papers discussing current applications and deployment experiences, and also the network layer communication and Quality of Service issues that are fundamental in further developing solutions to applications.

With contributions from researchers, this book strikes a balance between fundamental concepts and new technologies, providing readers with unprecedented insights into WSNs from a networking perspective. It is an essential reading for a broad audience, including academic researchers, research engineers, and practitioners in industry. The readership of this book is intended to be postgraduate/postdoctoral researchers, and professional engineers. It is also suitable as a textbook or supplementary reading for computer engineering and computer science courses at the graduate level.

January 2020

N. R. Shetty
Former Vice-Chancellor
Bangalore University
Bengaluru, India

Preface

Wireless Sensor Networks are composed of inexpensive, low powered micro-sensor nodes capable of sensing, processing, and communicating with limited computational resources. The sensor nodes organize themselves dynamically to form a network and communication is established between the nodes through broadcasting using radio signals. WSNs do not have a definite fixed infrastructure and hence the network topology changes continuously based on the type of sink, number of hops, types of nodes, and type of scheduling.

Wireless Sensor Networks basically keep track of the physical environment and co-operatively transmit data to the destination via the self organized network. A large amount of sensor nodes are widely deployed at high density regions where surveillance and monitoring is required, especially, at the frontiers of land, medical applications, commercial, industries, home automation, automobiles, chemical industries, in remote areas like forest, mountains, and valleys etc., where deployment of monitoring devices becomes impossible due to practical limitations. They can also be embedded in an environment to monitor variety of physical and environmental information, interact, assimilate, and interpret real time data in smart environmental applications. Emerging WSNs have a set of stringent Quality of Service (QoS) requirements that include timeliness, high reliability, availability, and integrity.

Chapter 1 introduces the basic idea of QoS in Wireless Sensor Networks and the unique design requirements and challenges for providing QoS in WSNs. The organization of the book is outlined in this chapter. QoS issues related to network layer and MAC layer routing are presented.

Chapter 2 presents Link Reliability based Two-Hop Routing (LRTHR) that explores the idea of incorporating Quality of Service parameters in making routing decisions, i.e., (i) reliability (ii) latency, and (iii) energy efficiency. The algorithm selects links providing greater Packet Reception Ratio (PRR) on the route, hence the throughput can be increased, lowering the Deadline Miss Ratio (DMR) and augmenting the energy efficiency of the forwarding nodes due to lower number of collisions and re-transmissions. The algorithm provides a two-hop neighborhood information scheme incorporated with the dynamic velocity assignment policy which provides enhanced foresight to the sender in identifying the node pair that can provide the largest velocity towards the destination.

In order to satisfy the QoS requirements and energy constraints for WSNs, hierarchical (clustering) techniques have been an attractive approach to organize sensor nodes based on their power levels and proximity. Chapter 3 proposes a Fault Tolerant QoS Adaptive Clustering Algorithm (FTQAC) that employs a dual cluster head mechanism in the cluster with respect to the working of the cluster head and guarantees the desired QoS by including delay and bandwidth parameters in the route selection process.

In order to sustain the QoS path when sensor nodes deteriorate and malfunction, node fault detection and recovery techniques are necessary. Expected Transmission Count and Round-Trip Time Delay (ETXTD) based Fault Detection Algorithm is explained in Chap. 4 that is able to identify working and faulty sensors in a computationally effective manner. The traffic is redirected to the working sensors and the QoS level is maintained throughout the duration of the connection.

Time synchronization is an important parameter for an event action, coordination among nodes and time measurements for common time on distributed sensor nodes. Chapter 5 proposes a Distributed QoS in Time Synchronized MAC (DQTSM) protocol that is a primary service for coordination of scattered sensor nodes regularly by exchanging messages in the WSNs applications in home automation, industrial automation, military, and medical etc. The DQTSM is important for the operation of WSNs in considering local clocks at each sensor node that need to be synchronized with reference to the clock at Master node. The synchronization error is due to the non-deterministic random time delay for a message transfer between the Master node and the Receiver nodes. DQTSM reduces sources of synchronization error at the MAC layer in channel contention and reduces the network traffic required for time synchronization.

Chapter 6 proposes an Efficient Retransmission Random Access Protocol (ERRAP) that retransmits a new frame within a pre-calculated time slot, which combines scheme of collision avoidance and energy management for low-cost, short-range wireless radios, and low-energy sensor nodes applications. This scheme focuses on efficient MAC scheme to provide autonomous Quality of Service (QoS) to the sensor nodes in one-hop QoS retransmission group in WSNs. The wireless sensor nodes joins the network only during random access time. The time interval between random access time could be small. Our simulation results demonstrate the performance of ERRAP protocol which increases the delivery probability and reduces the energy consumption.

It is challenging to design a hybrid MAC scheme for delay aware data traffic in WSNs. The Contention Based Hybrid MAC (CBH-MAC) protocol is proposed in Chap. 7, where each sensor node operates the reservation procedure used in cross and chain topology, resulting in energy efficiency, maximizing the packet delivery ratio, minimizing contention around the nodes, and reducing end-to-end delay. The neighboring sensor nodes of the receiver and sender receive their individual reservation control packets. The sender transmits data and receives Acknowledgment packets during the adaptive contention-free period. As the reservation packets pass through the sensor along the routing path, the sensor nodes reserve the time slots consecutively in multi-hop. The scheme has significant improvement of the end-to-end latency, packet delivery ratio, and energy efficiency.

Chapter 8 proposes a QoS Multi-hop Sensor Routing (QMSR) protocol that is developed for Mobile Wireless Sensor Networks (MWSNs). This protocol manages Admission Control Scheme (ACS) with minimum overhead resources for fresh flows without degrading the performance of the existing flows. ACS is an important strategy for regulating the parallel flows in a contention based channels to meet the requirements of QoS. QMSR estimates the available bandwidth before allocating the resources on a per hop basis. The protocol minimizes the overall energy consumption and guarantees the end-to-end delay.

Chapter 9 presents Passive Clustering. Passive Clustering does not employ control packets to collect topological information in a Mobile Wireless Sensor Network. In our proposal, we avoid making frequent changes in cluster architecture, due to repeated election and re-election of cluster heads and gateways. Our primary objective has been to make Passive Clustering more practical, robust and to minimize the quantity of cluster information on the data packets.

Chapter 10 proposes a Secure Aggregation for Approximate Queries in Wireless Sensor Networks (SAAQ) where Message Authentication Codes (MACs) are transmitted along with the synopses that are generated using primitive polynomials.

The authors appreciate the suggestions from the readers and users of this book. Kindly communicate the errors, if any, to the following e-mail address: venugopalkr@gmail.com.

Bengaluru, India   K. R. Venugopal
January 2020

Acknowledgements

We wish to place on record our deep debt of gratitude to Late Shri M. C. Jayadeva, Prof. K. Venkatagiri Gowda, Prof. P. Sreenivas Kumar for their inspiration, encouragement, and guidance throughout our lives. We thank Prof. N. R. Shetty, President, ISTE and Former Vice Chancellor, Bangalore University for his foreword to this book. We owe debt of gratitude to Prof. L. M. Patnaik, Sri K. Narahari, Sri V. Nagaraj, Prof. S. Lakshmana Reddy, Prof. K. Mallikarjuna Chetty, Prof. H. N. Shivashankar, Prof. Kamala Krithivasan, Prof. C. Sivarama Murthy, Prof. T. Basavaraju, Prof. M. Channa Reddy, Prof. N. Srinivasan, Prof. M. Venkatachalappa, T. G. Girikumar, P. Palani, M. G. Muniyappa for their support.

We are grateful to Justice M. Rama Jois, Sri Y. K. Raghavendra Rao, Sri Prabhakar Bhat, Prof. K. V. Acharya, Sri D. M. Ravindra, Sri Jagadeesh Karanath, Sri N. Thippeswamy, Sri Sudhir, Sri V. Manjunath, Sri N. Dinesh Hegde, Sri Nagendra Prasad, Smt. Karthyayini V, Tejaswi Venugopal, Sri K. Thyagaraj, Smt. Rukmini T., and Late Smt. Savithri Venkatagiri Gowda, our well wishers for their encouragement and inspiring us to write this book.

We thank, Dr. Dinesh Anvekar, Dr. P. Deepa Shenoy, Dr. K. B. Raja, Dr. K. Suresh Babu, Dr. D. N. Sujatha, Dr. Vibha L., Dr. S. H. Manjula, Dr. Thriveni J., Dr. Anita Kanavalli, Dr. Veena H. Bhat, Dr. Sivasankari H., Dr. Shaila K., Dr. Srikantaiah K. C., Dr. Prashanth C. R., Dr. Ramachandra, Smt. Nalini, Dr. D. Annapurna, Dr. Kumaraswamy M., Sri Girish K., Dr. Kiran K., Dr. Arunalatha J. S., Dr. Lata B. T., Smt. Gomathy Prathima Sejal Nimbhorkar, Raghevendra, Geeta M. C., Ramya, Roopa M. S., Santhosh Pattar Vandana Jha, Krishna Kumar N., Srikanth P. L., Suraj M., Roopa M. S., Shailesh Kumar Gupta, Kamalakant Tiwari, Vinuth Chandrashekar, Vijay Mathapati, Rashmi V., Abhishek Datta, Takur Ganesh Singh and Shradha G., and all the Research Scholars. We express our gratitude and heartfelt thanks to our family members Dr. T. Krishnaprasad, Smt. Harini S., Sri N. R. Harinath, Smt. H. Chandrakala, Sri Raghavendra Harinath, Smt. R. Anusha, and Master Anantha Vittala S.

Contents

About the Authors

Dr. K. R. Venugopal is the Vice Chancellor of Bangalore University. He holds eleven degrees, including a Ph.D. in Computer Science Engineering from IIT-Madras, Chennai and a Ph.D. in Economics from Bangalore University, as well as degrees in Law, Mass Communication, Electronics, Economics, Business Finance, Computer Science, Public Relations, and Industrial Relations.

Dr. Venugopal has authored and edited 68 books and published more than 800 papers in refereed international journals and conferences. Dr. Venugopal was a Postdoctoral Research Scholar at the University of Southern California, USA. He has been conferred IEEE fellow and ACM Distinguished Educator for his contributions to Computer Science Engineering and Electrical Engineering education.

Dr. Shiv Prakash T. is currently Director of the Vijaya Vittala Institute of Technology, Bangalore, India. He holds a Ph.D., M.S., and B.E. in Computer Science and Engineering from Bangalore University. He has over ten years of IT experience in the field of Embedded Systems and Digital Multimedia. He is currently authoring the book Mastering Java to be published in 2021. His research areas include Wireless Sensor Networks, Computer Vision, Embedded Linux, and Digital Multimedia.

Dr. M. Kumaraswamy is currently a Professor at the Department of Computer Science and Engineering at SJPT, Bangalore. He holds a Ph.D. in Computer Science and Engineering from JNTU Hyderabad, B.E. degree in Electrical and Electronics Engineering from the University of Mysore, Mysore, and M.Tech in System Analysis and Computer Applications from NITK Surathkal. His research interests include Wireless Sensor Networks and Adhoc Networks.

Acronyms

ACK	Acknowledgement
ACS	Admission Control Scheme
AIS	Artificial Immune System
AODV	Ad Hoc On-Demand Distance Vector
ARQ	Automatic Repeat Request
BS	Base Station
BWER	Bandwidth Efficiency Ratio
CACP	Contention-Aware Admission Control Protocol
CBR	Constant Bit Rate
CCBR	Context and Content-Based Routing
CDA	Concealed Data Aggregation
CDMA	Code Division Multiple Access
CDS	Connected Dominating Set
CP	Contention Period
CR	Cognitive Radio
CSMA	Carrier Sense Multiple Access
CSMA/CA	Carrier Sense Multiple Access/Collision Avoidance
CSMA/CD	Carrier Sense Multiple Access/Collision Detection
CTS	Clear To Send
DCA	Dynamic Channel Assignment
DCF	Distributed Coordination Function
DMR	Deadline Miss Ratio
DMST	Directed Minimum Spanning Tree
DRAND	Distributed Randomized
DSDV	Destination Sequenced Distance Vector
DSR	Dynamic Source Routing
E2E	End-to-End
ECC	Elliptic Curve Cryptography
ECPP	Energy Consumed Per Packet
ETX	Expected Transmission Count

EWMA	Exponential Weighted Moving Average
FBS	Feedback Based Synchronization
FCFS	First-Come-First-Served
FDMA	Frequency Division Multiple Access
FHSS	Frequency Hopping Spread Spectrum
FTSP	Flooding Time Synchronization Protocol
GPS	Global Positioning System
GPSR	Greedy Perimeter Stateless Routing
HMAC	Hash Message Authentication Code
H-MAC	Hybrid Medium Access Control
ISM	Industrial, Scientific and Medical
MAC	Medium Access Control
MAC	Message Authentication Code
MANET	Mobile Ad Hoc Network
MAP	Multi-channel Access Protocol
MC-LMAC	Multi-Channel Lightweight Medium Access Control
MEMS	Micro Electrical and Mechanical Systems
MFS	Multipath Fairness Solution
MILP	Mixed Integer Linear Programming
MMSN	Multi-FrequencyMedia Access Control
MQO	Modern Query Optimization
MSN	Mobile Sensor Node
MWSN	Mobile Wireless Sensor Network
NCP	Non Contention Period
NS	Network Simulator
ODI	Order and Duplicate Insensitive
OLSR	Optimized Link State Routing
OMC-MAC	Opportunistic Multi-Channel Medium Access Control
PAC	Perceptive Admission Control
PCH	Primary Cluster Head
PCSA	Probabilistic Counting with Stochastic Averaging
PDEM	Path-Demand Packet
PDR	Packet Delivery Ratio
PREP	Path-Reply
PREQ	Path-Request
PRR	Packet Reception Ratio
QoS	Quality-of-Service
RBS	Reference Broadcast Synchronization
RF	Radio Frequency
RMAC	Routing-Enhanced Medium Access Control
RMS	Root Mean Square
RN	Receiver Node
RPR	Regular Packet Rate
RRP	Resource Reservation Procedure
RSSI	Received Signal Strength Indicator

RT-LINK	Real Time Link
RTP	Round Trip Path
RTS	Request To Send
RTT	Round Trip Time
Rx	Receiver
SCH	Secondary Cluster Head
S-MAC	Sensor Medium Access Control
SRP-MS	Square Routing Protocol with Mobile Sink
TDMA	Time Division Multiple Access
TMCP	Tree-based Multi-Channel Protocol
TPSN	Timing-sync Protocol for Sensor Networks
TTL	Time to Live
TTS	Two-hop Time Synchronization
Tx	Transmiter
WMEWMA	Window Mean Exponential Weighted Moving Average
WSNs	Wireless Sensor Networks

Chapter 1
An Introduction to QoS in Wireless Sensor Networks

Wireless Sensor is deployed in an environment to monitor a physical phenomenon, collect data, execute light processes, and send either raw data or aggregate processed information to a destination. Usually, the number of sensor nodes is large and have a limited communication range. A message must be forwarded in multiple hops *via* neighboring nodes in order to reach the remote sink node. An example of a deployed Wireless Sensor Network is shown in Fig. 1.1. The base station is considered as a sink since it requires more power, resources, and an Internet connections. Each sensor node senses data from its surrounding environment, performs computation on the assimilated data, and forwards packets on behalf of each other to the desired destinations *via* neighboring nodes through radio links. WSNs play a central role in achieving the goal of truly ubiquitous computing and smart environments.

Wireless Sensor Networks are infra structureless networks. The topology of the WSNs is classified based on the

- *Type of Sink*: Multi-sink and Mobile sink. In *multi-sink*, more than one node is considered as the sink node and in *mobile sink*, the sink is considered to be moving.
- *Number of hops*: Single-hop for less coverage area, *Multi-hop* for large coverage area and Wireless Mesh Networks for very large coverage area.
- *Type of nodes*: Homogeneous type and Heterogeneous type. In a *homogeneous networks*, all the parameters and computation capabilities of the nodes remain the same whereas in *heterogeneous networks*, the parameters and computation capabilities of the nodes vary.
- *Type of scheduling*: Event-driven and time-driven sensor networks. In *event-driven* sensor networks, when an event occurs the nodes wake-up from sleep mode, senses the data, processes it and transmits to the sink; whereas in *time driven* networks, the nodes wake-up from the sleep mode only at specified intervals regularly, senses data, processes data and transmits to the sink.

Due to the infra structureless topology of WSNs, *connectivity* and *link* characteristic change regularly. There is an increasing demand for real-time applications that require certain End-to-End performance guarantees. In Real time communication, information is received at, or nearly at the moment it is sent. Real-time applications

© Springer Nature Singapore Pte Ltd. 2020
K. R. Venugopal et al., *QoS Routing Algorithms for Wireless Sensor Networks*,
https://doi.org/10.1007/978-981-15-2720-3_1

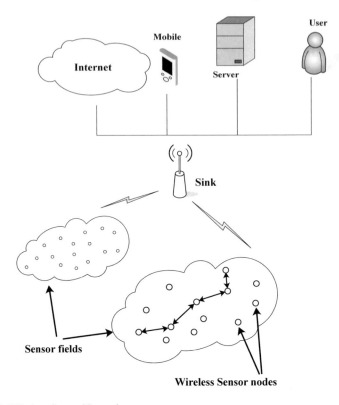

Fig. 1.1 Wireless Sensor Network

demand Quality of Service (QoS), in which there may be a scale of performance that
is acceptable for that application.

For example, in a WSN based video vigilance application, the user should be able
to view a certain video resolution without data delay. These user-level QoS demands
should be mapped to network level QoS parameters like bandwidth and delay. The
design of the application in this scheme is about providing information in a prompt,
reliable, and complete way. Moreover, the life span of the system as a whole should
be maximized, without replacing sensors.

However, satisfying the QoS requirements in a resource bounded environment
imposes new challenges to routing in WSNs. Most routing protocols focus on energy
consumption and ignore real-time communication or assume that the traffic speed
is sufficient to meet the QoS requirements. As a consequence, WSN applications
require routing techniques for different QoS requirements that consider reliability,
latency, network throughput, and power efficiency. These targets can be formalized
into QoS performance characteristics.

1.1 Wireless Sensor Network Architecture

A Wireless Sensor Network is a self-configuring network consisting of tiny autonomous devices called *sensor nodes* which communicate among themselves using radio signals. The nodes in the network perform different roles depending on their location in the network. The hardware of the sensor node consists of a power unit, sensing unit, processing unit, trans-receiver unit, and actuators [2].

1.1.1 Sensor Network Units

The most important units of the sensor network are

- *Sensor Node (Mote)*: A hardware device that causes measurable feedback to a change in physical or environmental conditions at different locations. Sensor nodes form a wireless network by communicating over a wireless medium. They are liable for collecting and routing data back to the sink.
- *Sink (Gateway)*: A special device that has more power than a sensor node and is responsible for sending collected data to the user. The sink is located near or inside the sensor field. It can be stationary or moving within the sensor field.
- *Sensor channels*: The communication channel among the sensor nodes and sink.
- *Network channels*: The transmission channel from the sensor network to other networks, or between different sensor networks.
- *Phenomenon*: A phenomenon is an event that is sensed, measured, monitored, and analyzed by the sensor nodes.
- *User*: The person interested in obtaining information about a specific phenomenon.

1.1.2 Sensor Node Hardware Architecture

The sensor nodes have various hardware modules that have specific roles in the functioning of the sensor device, the hardware architecture of a sensor node is shown in Fig. 1.2.

- The *Power Unit* supplies the necessary power to subsystems, from a battery or a solar module. In a sensor node, power is consumed by sensing, communication, and data processing. Extra power is required for data communication than for sensing and data processing. Power can be stored in batteries or capacitors. Batteries are the main source of power supply for sensor nodes. For example, Mica2 Mote runs on two AA batteries. Due to the finite capacity of batteries, minimizing energy consumption is always a key concern during WSN operations. Renewable energy techniques convert ambient energy (e.g., solar, wind) to electrical energy.

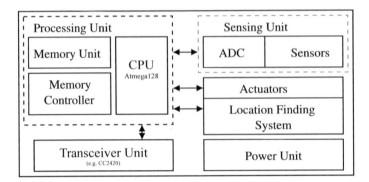

Fig. 1.2 Architecture of a sensor node

- The *Sensing Unit* includes analog sensors and Analog to Digital Converters which sample the data and deliver to the processing unit, this module usually has multiple sensors. A sensor produces a response signal to a change in temperature, pressure, and light. The continuous analog signal is sensed and digitized by an ADC and sent to the embedded processor for processing. By virtue of its limited power source, the attached sensors should also be miniature in size and consume low energy. A sensor can have one or several types of sensors combined in or linked to the node.
- The *Processing Unit* controls the operations of the sensor. In a sensor node, the purpose of an embedded processor is to lineup tasks, process data, and control other hardware components. The various embedded processors that can be used in a sensor node include Microcontroller, Digital Signal Processor, and Application Specific Integrated Circuit. The Microcontroller has been extensively used for sensor nodes because of its ability to connect to other devices and its low price.
- The *Memory Unit* saves program code and data. Memories in a sensor node have in-chip flash memory and RAM of a microcontroller and external flash memory. For example, the ATMega128L microcontroller running on Mica2 Mote has 4-Kbyte static RAM and 128-Kbyte flash program memory.
- The *Transceiver Unit* facilitates the communications with other sensor nodes. A transceiver is liable for the wireless communication of a sensor node. The different choices of wireless transmission media include radio frequency and infrared. Radio frequency-based communication is used in most of WSN applications. The working modes of a transceiver are Transmit, Receive, Idle, and Sleep.
- *Actuators Unit* is responsible for moving, controlling speed and direction of the mobile sensor nodes.
- The *Location finding device* is a GPS unit.
- The *Operating System (OS)* role is to encourage the development of dependable application software by providing a comfortable and safe abstraction of the hardware. Operating systems for WSN nodes are simpler than general purpose operating systems both because of the special requirements of WSN applications and constraints in WSN hardware platforms. TinyOS is the first operating system spe-

cially designed for WSNs. TinyOS has been ported to over many platforms and numerous sensor boards. WSN project developers worldwide use this operating system in simulation to develop and test various algorithms and protocols.

1.1.3 Sensor Wireless Stack and Standards

The 802.15.4 and Zigbee are the two wireless standards used by WSNs [3]. IEEE 802.15.4 network operates in one of the three Industrial, Scientific, and Medical (ISM) frequency bands. The channel width is 2.40–2.483 GHz, 16 channels with a bit rate of 868–868.6 MHz for 20/100/250 Kb/s or 902.0–928.0 MHz for 40/280 Kb/s and 2.40–2.483 GHz for 280 Kb/s of maximum output power 1000 mW as per Federal Commission of Communications (FCC). The companies manufacturing WSNs are Moog CrossBow, Sentilla based on Java and Libeliumbenet on Arduino and Open Source Software (Zigbee) [4].

The protocol stack used by Wireless Sensor Network [2] is given in Fig. 1.3. This protocol stack blends power and routing awareness, combines data with networking protocols, conveys power efficiently through the wireless medium, and builds cooperative efforts of sensor nodes. The WSN protocol stack contains the following layers Application, Transport, Network, Data Link, Physical and planes such as Power Management, Mobility Management, and Task Management [5]. As per the sensing tasks, different types of application software can be developed and used on the application layer. The transport layer helps to manage the data flow. The network layer routes the data supplied by the transport layer. The WSN environment is noisy

Fig. 1.3 Wireless Sensor Network stack model

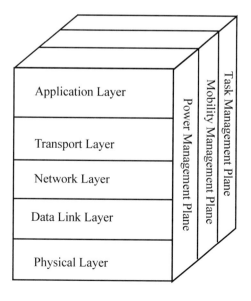

and sensor nodes can be mobile, hence the MAC protocol must be power-aware and be able to minimize collision with neighbor broadcasts. The physical layer addresses the needs of a simple but sturdy modulation, transmission, and receiving methods. The power, mobility, and task management planes supervise the power, movement, and task distribution among the sensor nodes. The planes aid the sensor nodes to coordinate the sensing function and reduce the overall power consumption.

1.2 Network Layer Issues and Challenges

1.2.1 Limitations of Wireless Sensor Networks

    (i) Adaptability.
   (ii) Data Processing.
  (iii) Energy Consumption caused due to collisions, overhearing, control packet overhead, idle listening, periodic listening.
  (iv) High Latency in communication is caused due to multi-hops and network congestion.
   (v) Limited Bandwidth.
  (vi) Localization and Network Topology.
 (vii) Media Access Control (MAC).
(viii) Operation in hostile environment.
  (ix) Routing Algorithm for Energy Aware Routing.
   (x) Scalability of Network size.
  (xi) Unstructured and time-varying network topology.
 (xii) Unreliable Communications since routing is based on connectionless protocols.

1.2.2 Challenges of Wireless Sensor Networks

    (i) Connectivity.
   (ii) Coverage.
  (iii) Data Aggregation.
  (iv) Data Mining with respect to distributed sensor networks.
   (v) Fault Tolerance.
  (vi) Heterogeneous environment.
 (vii) Large Scale Deployment.
(viii) Mobility of nodes.
  (ix) Multimedia Applications.
   (x) Multiple QoS levels.
  (xi) Multiple sink nodes.

   (xii) Network Dynamics.
  (xiii) Node failure.
  (xiv) Quality of Service of the network.
   (xv) Security.
  (xvi) Self-configuration.
 (xvii) Transmission Media.
(xviii) Unattended Operations.
  (xix) Untethered.

1.3 Medium Access Control Layer Issues and Challenges

1.3.1 Issues of Medium Access Control MAC Layer

The communication challenges in WSNs occur from low-bandwidth, high node density, low energy device, sensing capability of small power transceivers, hardware limitations and computational power [6]. The architecture of WSNs should be simple in order to minimize the influence of communication. Thus, the majority of WSNs are designed as one hop topology since multi-hop topology has high demands on the routing protocol and the bandwidth requirements.

   (i) *Packet/Frame Collision*: The packet/frame collision occurs when two or more packets/frames are transmitted at the same time, gets corrupted due to interference and hence discarded. As a result, the retransmission of packet/frame increases energy consumption.

  (ii) *Overhearing*: A node picks up frames/packets that are intended to other nodes. In WSNs, under heavy load environments, sensor networks overlap since the sensing ranges of many wireless physical sensors are much smaller than the communication range.

 (iii) *Packet/Frame Overhead*: Packet/frame overhead is the energy consumed by exchanging control packets. The packet/frame overhead is necessary to avoid collision and share wireless medium in WSNs.

 (iv) *Idle Listening*: In WSNs, one of the sources of inefficiency is idle listening. The wireless sensor node keeps listening even when there is no transmission for most of the time. This is due to the Medium Access Control protocols that avoid frequent switching, leaving the radio transceiver module in idle listening state.

  (v) *Time Synchronization*: Most of the Wireless Sensor Network applications require time synchronization. In order to preserve energy, each sensor node radio may be turned on or off for some periods of time. Sensor nodes may compute the delay of a data frame as it travels between the nodes and may require group synchronization for target tracking applications.

 (vi) *Retransmission*: Retransmission is one of the most popular mechanisms to improve the transmission reliability in WSNs, where the source node after transmitting its message, waits for the acknowledgment from the sink. However, in case the source sensor nodes do not accept any acknowledgments, it assumes that the sent data is lost. Thus, in order to ensure reliability, the lost message needs to be retransmitted.

(vii) *End-to-End Delay*: The time required to transfer a data frame/packet from the source sensor node to the destination node is termed as end-to-end delay. In real-time applications, WSNs require guaranteed QoS for delivering data. The performance of end-to-end delay is required, suitable to the non-deterministic collisions of the radio channel and in evaluating QoS based multi-hop scheme.

(viii) *Admission Control*: In WSNs, the admission control at medium access control is the amount of data in which a node may send in a given time period. It may determine the number of bytes it can allow from source sensor node to destination node. Admission control handles requests of sensor nodes and maintains the QoS for the admitted sensor nodes to use the wireless channel.

1.3.2   MAC Scheme Design Challenges

The design of the MAC scheme is a challenge for WSNs due to the dense network design of sensor nodes, energy limitations, and low transmission ranges. The Medium Access Control protocol for the WSNs has to successfully complete two important goals. Firstly, the formation of the wireless sensor network infrastructure. The MAC protocols must set up the communication channel among all the sensor nodes. The next goal is to allocate the communication resources efficiently and fairly.

In WSNs averting collisions is an important role that MAC plays to enhance the network performance. MAC protocols augment reliability with acknowledgment messages and retransmissions. Limitations coming from environmental factors and hardware equipment demand precise MAC protocols.

To design a desired Medium Access Control scheme for the WSNs, the following metrics have to be considered.

(i) *Energy Efficiency*: This is an important parameter in the WSNs. A wireless sensor node is equipped with a processor, sensors with limited computation power, small radio range, and an irreplaceable battery.

(ii) *Latency*: Latency depends on the sensor application and the node state. In the WSNs applications, the sensing events are reported to the destination node. Hence, appropriate action needs to be taken immediately.

(iii) *Throughput*: It is defined as the quantity of data successfully transferred from the sender node to the receiver node by a wireless communication channel. It is typically calculated as message transmission for every second. The main purpose of a Medium Access Control scheme is to increase the wireless channel throughput while decreasing packet/frame transmission period.

(iv) *Fairness*: In a number of WSN applications, bandwidth is the constraint; each sensor node requires equal opportunity to access the medium among the competing nodes. The sink node should receive information fairly from all the sensor nodes. Fairness between all the competing nodes is useful for QoS requirements that result in energy efficiency and high throughput.

(v) *Scalability*: It is related to the ability of the communication system to accommodate a larger network, that is more number of competing sensor nodes and topology of the wireless network.

1.4 MAC Scheme in Wireless Sensor Networks

MAC scheme for WSNs have to deal with a broad range of challenges. The MAC schemes have to be optimized in terms of computational power, maximize throughput, minimize delay, and must be energy efficient. Wireless communication is often unreliable due to the limited transmission range of the chip antennas, weak transmission power. Event-driven and highly correlated traffic, frequent synchronization due to high clock drift of microcontrollers and battery power constraints.

The nodes are generally built of low price hardware to decrease the prices of WSNs. The high node density intensifies the crisis of medium access in WSNs further. The synchronization of a huge number of nodes is a significant task. An account of the high clock drift of the microcontrollers, regular resynchronization is required which consumes high computational power and energy.

The Medium Access Control protocols are classified into three categories based on the medium access method: (i) Contention-free, (ii) Contention-based and (iii) Hybrid-based access mechanisms. In a contention-free mechanism, sensor networks schedule the channel, either in time or frequency, where nodes can only access their allocated carrier slots and thus communicate with the sink node in a collision-free manner. In contention-based sensor networks, nodes contend with each other to access the wireless medium. The Hybrid MAC protocols combine the above two schemes.

1.4.1 Contention-Free MAC Protocols

In contention-free based MAC protocol, nodes only awaken and listen to the carrier in allocated time slots and then return to sleep in other time slots. The advantages of contention-free based schemes include no collisions, avoidance of idle listening, and less overhearing. Additionally, it has a predictable and bounded end-to-end delay. However, the average queuing delay is much higher and nodes have to wait for the allocated time slot before accessing the carrier. The high-load traffic is suitable for contention-free based MAC protocols [7].

1.4.2 Contention MAC Protocols

The contention-based MAC scheme competes with its neighboring node to access the wireless carrier. Initially, before any transmission take place, a node having a frame/packet for transmission senses the carrier. If the node finds the carrier idle, the node starts transmitting. Otherwise, it postpones the transmission for some random time determined by a back-off algorithm. In general, sensor nodes contend for the wireless carrier and only the successful node is permitted to access the carrier and transmit. One of the most significant strengths of the contention-based Medium Access Control scheme is that it is a fairly simple method compared to the contention-free based scheme since it does not require either global synchronization or topology knowledge. However, conventional contention-based MAC scheme is not appropriate for most of the WSNs applications because of low energy efficiency.

1.4.3 Hybrid MAC Protocols

The advantages of both contention-free and contention-based Medium Access Control protocols are combined in Hybrid-based MAC protocols. The hybrid-based MAC schemes are of two categories (i) combination of the contention-free and (ii) partition access mechanism [8]. In reservation-for-contention MAC, the nodes describe familiar wake-up or sleep times. The wake-up slots are used for communication channel and the sleep slots are used for saving energy. In this approach, the sensor nodes need to maintain synchronization to remain in wake-up or sleep times common to all nodes that are similar to contention-free MAC. However, the use of regular wake-up or sleep times may not be appropriate for applications with regular traffic or high traffic load. Contention-based protocols suit low traffic loads while contention-free based scheme is a better choice for high traffic.

1.5 Motivation

1.5.1 Network Layer

Emerging WSNs have a set of stringent QoS requirements that include timeliness, high reliability, availability, and integrity. The competence of a WSN lies in its ability to provide these QoS requirements. The timeliness and reliability level for data exchanged between sensors and control station is of paramount importance, especially in real time scenarios. The Deadline Miss Ratio (DMR), defined as the ratio of packets that cannot meet the end-to-end deadline should be minimized. Sensor nodes typically use batteries for energy supply. Hence, energy efficiency and load balancing form important objectives while designing QoS protocols for WSNs.

Cluster heads provide optimization capabilities like data fusion and communication using TDMA. In clustering high power nodes can be used to process sensed data and communicate with other nodes, while low power nodes are used for sensing. The clustering technique is a good way to achieve higher energy efficiency, longer lifetime, and scalability The QoS of the network can be improved by considering fault tolerance and bandwidth in the protocol metrics.

Several factors, such as the random nature of the communication channel, collision, congestion, and presence of interference, affect the reliability in Wireless Sensor Networks. Current works attempt to enhance reliability by packet loss avoidance and packet loss recreation techniques which can be achieved in a per-hop or end-to-end method. These recovery techniques have practical problems that include long transmission paths, radio interference, packet collisions, and bad link propagation due to broken links. These techniques perform well in a small network but when the network size scales up, their effectiveness in improving the reliability is diminished due to collisions and congestion.

The QoS of the network is damaged by the failure of sensor nodes. The probability of sensor node failure raises with more sensors. In order to maintain QoS paths under failure conditions, locating and detaching such faults becomes important. The goal is to design algorithms that are capable of providing QoS to the applications with minimum energy consumption.

1.5.2 Medium Access Control Layer

Synchronization is not needed in the centralized system as there is no ambiguity in time. Absence of common memory and a global clock is a fundamental characteristic of distributed systems. Each sensor node has its individual notion of time and owns internal clock. These clocks drift several seconds per day and can accumulate significant errors over time. The protocol that runs in a densely distributed system needs to record time in one or more aspects as follows: (i) Time of occurrence of an event, (ii) Time interval between occurrence of two events and (iii) Relative time of the occurrence of events on different sensor nodes in the WSNs.

In applications of sensor networks, sensor node data must be delivered to the destination node within the specified time. It is essential to evaluate the performance metrics, such as the consumption of energy and maximum data delivery of traffic loads under all circumstances. Hence, optimization of the packet delivery probability and energy efficiency has to be planned while designing WSNs.

Existing Medium Access Control protocols for WSNs are classified into three groups: (a) contention-based protocols (b) schedule based protocols and (c) hybrid protocols. For delay-sensitive applications Hybrid MAC can use channel reservation method to reduce end-to-end delay. The design of robust contention-free access time and contention-based reservation is paramount to handle fluctuating traffic load in WSNs.

The concept of Multi-channel MAC schemes is conceptualized for increasing the capacity of wireless access techniques. In Multi-channel access, wireless links can service different transmissions maintained simultaneously without collision. Multi-channel scheduling MAC assignment can remove the interference among different channels and result in collision-free transmission in the MAC layer. Here, each node can only transmit at the pre-assigned set of slots. The collision avoidance technique improves effective channel utilization, saving energy due to lower retransmission and higher delivery ratio. The Admission Control Scheme (ACS) determines whether the available resource in WSNs can allow new streams without affecting the Quality of Service of the existing streams.

1.5.3   Design and Evaluation Metrics in the Network Layer

The design of efficient routing protocols in WSNs are characterized by specific metrics such as Reliability, Bandwidth, End-to-End Delays, Reception Ratios, Throughput and Network Lifetime.

- *Bandwidth* is the capacity of the channel between the sender and receiver.
- *End-to-End Reliability* is the successful end-to-end transmission success rate *i.e.*, ratio of the successfully delivered packets to the total number of packets between the source and destination.
- *Packet End-to-End Delay* is the average and worst-case delays defined by the mean of packet delay and the largest value experienced by the successfully transmitted packets between source and destination.
- *Energy Consumed per Packet (ECPP)* is defined by the total energy consumed divided by the number of packets successfully transmitted.
- *Energy Efficiency* is the ratio of the end-to-end transmission success rate and the energy cost scaled by the minimum number of hops from node to sink.
- *Expected Transmission Count metric (ETX)* of a link is the predicted number of data transmissions required to send a packet over that link, including retransmissions.
- *Jitter* is referred to as variations in delay.
- *Network lifetime* is the time period of network being active.
- *Packet Deadline Miss Ratio (DMR)* is defined by the number of packets that miss their deadlines over the number of initiated packets.
- *Packet Reception Ratio (PRR)* denotes the probability of successful delivery over a link, i.e., ratio of the number of packets received to the total number of packets between two nodes.
- *Throughput* is the number of packets of user data transferred over some time interval.

1.5.4 Design and Evaluation Metrics in the Medium Access Layer

The performance parameters that can be satisfied at the MAC layer and the cross-layer are as follows:

- *Minimizing Channel Access Delay*: The network layer should manage the end-to-end delay from the source node to the destination sink node. The channel access delay can be minimized at the MAC layer to reduce the latency of packets and ensure the end-to-end delay.
- *Minimizing Collisions*: The Networking metrics such as delay, throughput, and energy efficiency are governed by collisions and subsequent retransmissions. Typically, the MAC layer determines the sharing of the channel, minimizes the number of collisions, by appropriate carrier sensing mechanism, and suitable contention window in the contention-based protocols. Similarly, an appropriate number of time periods and frequencies according to the wireless network conditions can avoid collisions during the contention-free scheme.
- *Maximizing Reliability*: MAC layer can also achieve its reliability by minimizing the collisions. The packet/frame losses can be recorded by appropriate acknowledgment techniques so that retransmissions can be minimized.
- *Minimizing Consumption of Energy*: It is the most critical requirement in WSNs on account of battery-powered operations of the sensor nodes. MAC layer can contribute to energy efficiency in MAC layer by decreasing collisions and retransmissions. The duty cycle is an important factor in WSN as the wireless operations consume most of the battery energy and the radio signal should be in a sleep state when the sensors are in the idle state.
- *Minimizing Interference*: As the wireless channel is a common medium, all unwanted transmissions in the network commencing from other networks that allocate the identical parts of the spectrum give rise to interference on the planned transmissions. Interference causes frame/packet losses and thus affects the throughput, energy efficiency and delay in the WSNs.
- *Maximizing Concurrent Transmissions*: Maximizing concurrent transmissions by limiting the impact of interference on concurrent transmissions. MAC layer can attain negligible interference and maximum concurrency as a result of alteration of the related parameters, for example, timing, contention windowing, transmission control, and working channel.
- *Synchronization*: In the design of WSNs, Time synchronization should be considered with the limited energy resources available in the sensor nodes. The accuracy and precision may change significantly depending on the synchronization of the specific WSNs applications. The time synchronization process of sensor nodes in WSNs should be designed with limited size and cost.

- *Retransmission*: Retransmission is one of the most popular mechanisms to improve the transmission reliability in WSNs, where the source nodes after transmitting its message, waits for the acknowledgment from the sink. However, if the source sensor node does not receive any acknowledgment, it assumes that the sent data has been lost. Thus, in order to ensure reliability, the lost message needs to be retransmitted.

1.6 Applications of Wireless Sensor Networks

WSNs can be used in many applications for uninterrupted sensing, event detection, and location sensing. The applications in WSNs can be broadly categorized into military, medical, commercial applications, and environmental. Some of these applications need real-time communication to deliver data on demand.

(i) *Military Applications*: WSNs form a fundamental part of military control and battlefield surveillance and are also used for detecting chemical, biological, radiological, and nuclear radiations [9]. The fast distribution and fault resilience nature of WSNs makes them a promising asset for the military. Sensors could be spread out in a hostile area to gather data about enemy troops, i.e., their ammunition, strength, and their current location. Data from sensor networks can be delivered to an intelligent system that can develop a battle plan. Sensors could also be used in a target area after the attack, to assess the damage.

(ii) *Environmental Applications*: Environment monitoring is another field where WSNs have been used to a great extent; some of the examples are, forest fire detection, landscape flooding alarm, pollution monitoring, irrigation, microclimate monitoring, solar radiation mapping, and bio-complexity mapping of the environment [10]. All the above examples are mostly large scale applications; smart homes and buildings can be considered as an example of small scale environmental monitoring [11, 12].

(iii) *Health Care and Medical applications*: WSNs play a vital role in monitoring patients to identify and resolve various life threatening health problems [13, 14]. Sensors are available for measuring blood flow, respiratory rate, ECG (Electrocardiogram), pulse oxymeter, blood pressure, and oxygen measurement. Smart sensors are placed in intensive care rooms to detect a fall or inactivity of patients. The data received can be known locally or the on-call nurse may know about their patient status for the nurse station. This type of medical application desires the WSNs to support and provide real-time information.

(iv) *Commercial applications*: WSNs find wide applications in the commercial areas for checking material fatigue, monitoring product quality, and automation [15, 16]. In a typical industrial system, sensor devices track manufacturing processes or the state of equipment through vibrations, heat, pressure levels, wear, and lubrication levels by placing sensors into regions inaccessible by humans. The sensor devices transmit this information to a control system. An industrial control system allows automated, accurate, factory process control that could not be achieved by human interaction. Hence, this aids to prevent imminent failures, or assist in performing preventive maintenance. Sensor networks have been extensively used for vehicle traffic monitoring and detecting car thefts. Video cameras are often used to monitor roads with heavy traffic and estimate their numbers and speed. In the automobile industry, WSNs are used to measure and notify users about critical parameters such as acceleration, fuel consumption, and other engine parameters [17].

1.7 Quality of Service in Wireless Sensor Networks

1.7.1 Introduction

Quality of Service can be defined as a set of service that needs to be satisfied when transporting a packet from the source to its destination and this translates to a networking QoS aspect, which requires the underlying network to provide a set of service attributes such as jitter, delay, bandwidth, and packet loss to monitor the service quality. The two broad QoS perspectives are Network QoS and Application QoS, as shown in Fig. 1.4 [18]. In this model, the application/users require the network to provide the required service quality. In turn, the network layer provides the required QoS level while maximizing network resource utilization; further the network analyzes the application requirements and deploys various network QoS mechanisms. The key issues to achieve QoS are (i) Reducing End-to-End delay (ii) Improving the End-to-End Reliability (iii) Reducing the packet Deadline Miss Ratio (DMR) (iv) Minimizing the Bandwidth utilization and (iv) Providing better energy utilization and load balancing among the sensors. (v) Minimizing Channel Access Delay. (vi) Minimizing Collisions (vii) Minimizing Interference. (viii) Maximizing Concurrent Transmissions.

Fig. 1.4 QoS Model

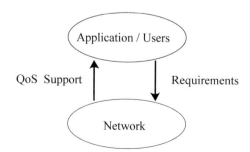

1.8   Quality of Service Architecture

1.8.1   Network and MAC Layer QoS Challenges

The unique requirements of WSNs pose new challenges for QoS design. The most predominant factors that need to be addressed in order to achieve effective real-time communication are

(i) *Bandwidth Constraint*: Bandwidth is the rate of data transfer. Sensors have very scarce bandwidth; if the load exceeds the available bandwidth, the network must respond by either discarding packets or queuing them in memory. Also, dedication of the entire bandwidth to real-time data that requires QoS is not acceptable. Hence, bandwidth allocation has to be carefully moderated.

(ii) *Buffer Size Constraint*: Buffer size plays an important role in storing the data before forwarding it to the next node. Multi-hop routing of QoS data requires lengthy sessions and buffering of data. The buffer size increases the delay difference that packets incur while traversing different routes.

(iii) *Data Redundancy*: High redundancy in the generated data is a characteristic of Wireless Sensor Networks. Aggregation and data fusion methods may complicate QoS design in multimedia WSNs.

(iv) *Multiple Sinks*: Recent WSNs have made use of multiple sinks to improve the reliability of the routing protocols. Sensor networks should be capable of supporting different QoS levels associated with multiple sinks.

(v) *Multiple Traffic Types*: The heterogeneous sensor networks can create challenges for multiple traffic QoS support. Transport of multiple types of sensed data at different rates makes QoS support more challenging.

(vi) *Network Dynamics*: Network dynamics may emerge from node failures, wireless link failures, node mobility, and node state. This often increases the complexity of QoS support.

(vii) *Queuing Constraint*: There are different types of queues available, such as Priority, FIFO, Weighted Fair queues, etc. Based on the hardware limitations of the sensor node, an appropriate queue has to be selected. Data packets may have different priorities. QoS mechanisms may be required to differentiate packet importance and set up a priority structure.

(viii) *Packet Criticality*: There are two kinds of packets, high priority and low priority packets. QoS mechanisms may be required to differentiate packet importance and set up a priority scheme.

(ix) *Resource Limitations*: Wireless Sensor Networks have very severe constraints on resources such as energy, memory, processing power, and buffer size. QoS mechanisms for WSNs should be designed in a manner avoiding computation intensive algorithms that drain selective nodes.

(x) *Scalability*: Scalability is the ability to maintain performance characteristics irrespective of the size of the network. With WSNs potentially consisting of thousands of nodes, in addition to the periodically added groups of nodes, scalability is an important issue.

(xi) *Unbalanced traffic*: All data from source nodes converge at the sink nodes, hence QoS mechanism should be designed for unbalanced traffic.

1.8.2 Network and MAC Layer QoS Requirements

Wireless Sensor Networks need better QoS so that any information communicated can be delivered in real time.

(i) *Self-Organization*: Sensor nodes have the ability to organize themselves in a hierarchical structure and be able to continue working even if one or more nodes fail.

(ii) *Low Latency*: Some applications require the delivery of data packets in real time and ensure binding deadlines. The latency of data packets include processing, queuing, transmission, and propagation delay. The processing delay is the time sensors take to decode the packet header, while the queuing delay is the time the packet resides in sensor queues. The transmission delay is the time it takes to transfer the packet's bits onto the link. The propagation delay is the time it takes for the signal to travel through the transmission medium. Timeliness can be provided either in an assured or a maximum effort basis as per the endurance level of applications.

(iii) *High Reliability*: It is defined in terms of the ability to deliver data to the destination with minimum packet loss. To assure such a lossless data transaction, prioritized forwarding or multi-path routing can be followed. Duplicating the same packet over different paths increases the probability that at least one of the copies arrives at the base station correctly. Unreliability of the wireless link is chiefly due to interference and congestion, reliability metric is often considered as complementary to the packet loss rate metric.

(iv) *Fault Tolerance*: Is defined as the capability to sustain the operations of the sensor network without any stoppage due to deterioration of the sensor node that happens due to lack of power, damage or network communication problems.

(v) *Minimal Bandwidth*: Real-time sensor applications have high bandwidth requirements. Due to the nature of multi-hop communication nodes relay packets for themselves and other nodes. An application should not allocate entire bandwidth to real-time data and a balance needs to be maintained. Therefore, high bandwidth demands should be taken into account when designing routing protocols for QoS WSNs.

(vi) *Energy Efficiency*: WSNs are battery-operated devices and power consumption of the communication module is higher. The transmission power of the sensor node is finite and the use of multi-hop routing is the most accepted technique in WSN data communication. Despite, the use of multi-hop routing which decreases energy consumption of individual nodes during transmission, it increases latency in end-to-end packet transfer. The increase in delay is mostly due to packet queuing at multiple sensor nodes and, therefore, it clouds the analysis and handling of QoS constrained traffic. To increase the lifetime of the network, energy utilization must be evenly distributed among all sensor nodes so that the energy at a single sensor node or a small set of sensor nodes is not depleted rapidly. QoS support should take these factors into account.

(vii) *Channel Capacity*: Capacity and delay feasible on each link are location reliant, and fluctuate frequently. Sensor data is commonly bandwidth intense, delay intolerant, and bursty. Hence, routing paths should be designed in such a way so that data can be disseminated in a balanced and energy-efficient way throughout the network under dynamic channel conditions.

(viii) *Hole Detection and Bypassing*: Due to the high bandwidth demands, some paths in WSNs can get depleted, these conditions are called dynamic holes. These holes may damage the performance of QoS applications by overburdening some routing paths. Hence, new hole bypassing routing methods should be designed to ease the streaming of data while balancing the energy usage all over the whole network.

(ix) *Scalability*: Scalability is the capability to preserve performance characteristics regardless of the size of the network. Sensor network is composed of thousands of individual sensors densely spread in the environment. Hence, QoS algorithms designed for WSNs should be able to scale up to a massive number of nodes. Moreover, scalability provides durability and fault tolerance for the network.

(x) *Reduced Data Redundancy*: High superfluity in the generated data is an aspect of Wireless Sensor Networks. Data fusion and aggregation functions are used to eliminate redundant data. These heavy computations often increase latency and hence make QoS design in WSNs challenging.

(xi) *Multiple Traffic Types*: In QoS Sensor networks, data propagated may have varied deadline requirements. Data generated from these sensors can be at contrasting rates, subject to varied QoS constraints and having multiple data delivery models. QoS algorithms may be required to differentiate packet emphasis and set up a precedence structure. Priority schemes can be enforced to differentiate among different types of data.

(xii) *Multiple Sinks*: Multiple sinks in the sensor network helps in reducing the congestion caused using a single destination. Multiple sinks help in improving the fault tolerance of the network. WSNs should also be able to handle different types of QoS levels associated with different sinks.

(xiii) *Minimal Jitter*: Jitter is specified as the accepted variations in delay. Typically for sensor traffic, each packet is assumed to have a normal jitter requirement. Random and deterministic are two types of jitter. The existence of jitter in transmission can cause glitches, disruption, and errors in data which is unacceptable in some applications where timely and exact delivery of information is imperative.

(xiv) *Availability*: Whenever an application requires service, the complete network or at least a group of sensor nodes should take the responsibility of providing the service even in the presence of node failures.

(xv) *Resilience to Failures*: Ability to withstand the network functionality when a portion of the nodes are malfunctioning or dead.

Although QoS have many design objectives, it is certainly impractical to design a routing approach that addresses all the objectives and requirements. QoS routing protocol design and implementations should focus on application-specific objectives and redesign the various layer as per requirements.

1.9 Software Tools

Some of the tools that can be used to simulate WSNs are ns-2, MATLAB, OMNeT++, TOSSIM, PC emulator XMOS, custom packet level simulator. The operating system that can be used on motes are LINUX, TinyOS, BerthaOS, EYESOS, MOS, BTnodes, Sensorware, MagnetOS, Mate, MiLAN, Middleware, SINA, TinyDB, LIME *etc*. The networks can be modeled using node system design tools. The Wireless Sensor Networks simulation and evaluation are categorized into Network Simulators with Node Models (NSNM), Network Simulators with Node Emulators (NSNE), Node System Simulator with Network Models (NSSNM), and Node Emulators with Network Models (NENM) as described in [19].

For the various network simulations, we have used ns-2 and LINUX scripts for the evaluation purpose, ns-2 is a discrete event, object-oriented, general purpose network simulator [20], hosting a rich set of Internet Protocols. It uses two languages: C++ and Object-oriented Tcl (OTcl). C++ is used for coding the routing protocols and Tcl is used to construct and control the simulation environment. The disadvantage of ns-2 is that it does not scale well in terms of memory usage and simulation time. [19]. Ns-2 provides substantial support for simulation of TCP, routing, and multicast protocols over wired and wireless (local and satellite) networks.

1.10 Organization of the Book

The book is organized into the following chapters. Chapter one gives a brief introduction to Wireless Sensor Networks and the QoS issues. Stateless Real-Time Two-Hop Routing is presented in Chapter two. Chapter three discusses Fault Tolerant Clustering in Wireless Sensor Networks. In chapter four, an algorithm for fault detection and detachment of defective nodes has been presented and evaluated. Simulations have been carried out to verify these concepts.

Algorithms for Distributed QoS in Time Synchronized MAC protocol is presented in chapter five. An algorithm for Efficient Retransmission QoS Aware MAC Protocol is presented in Chapter six. Contention-based Hybrid MAC protocol for multi-hop QoS in terms of self-configuration of the nodes is discussed in Chapter seven. In Chapter eight, an algorithm for Admission Control Scheme that can accommodate fresh flows without affecting the QoS of offered flows has been discussed.

Chapter nine shows that Passive Clustering becomes practically possible by implementing the intelligent gateway selection heuristic and on demand timeout mechanism. Frequent changes in cluster architecture are avoided by precluding repeated re-election of cluster heads. Chapter thirteen proposes a topology control energy management to increase the lifetime and QoS of the network. The flow requests are initially routed on short edges even though they utilize slightly higher energy. We have examined the MILP model based on multi commodity flow concept which involves splitting and re-routing the non-optimal flows over multiple paths.

Chapter ten proposes a Secure Aggregation for Approximate Queries in Wireless Sensor Networks (SAAQ) where Message Authentication Codes (MACs) are transmitted along with the synopses that are generated using primitive polynomials.

References

1. F.L. Lewis, D.J. Cook, S.K. Dasm, John Wiley: Wireless Sensor Networks, in *Proc. Smart Environment Technologies, Protocols and Applications* (New York, 2004), pp. 1–18
2. M. Kuorilehto, M. Hannikainen, T.D. Hamalainen, A survey of application distribution in wireless sensor networks. EURASIP J. Wireless Commun. Netw. **5**, 774–788 (2005)
3. X. Fafoutis, Introduction to wireless sensor networks, in *DTU Informatics, Department of Informatics and Mathematical Modeling*, Courses 02234 (2007)
4. M. Zennaro, A. Bagula, Introduction to wireless sensor networks, in *A Three Day Outreach Workshop in Wireless Sensor Networking and Environment Monitoring* (2011)
5. Y. Al-Obaisat, R. Braun, On wireless sensor networks: architectures, protocols, applications and management, in *Proceedings of Aus Wireless: International Conference on Wireless Broadband and Ultra Wideband Communication* (2006), pp. 1–6
6. I. Demirkol, C. Ersoy, F. Alagoez, MAC protocols for wireless sensor networks: a survey. IEEE Commun. Mag. **44**(4), 115–121 (2006)
7. V. Rajendran, K. Obraczka, J.J. Garcia-Luna-Aceves, Energy-efficient collision-free medium access control for wireless sensor networks, in *ACM SenSys* (2003), pp. 181–192
8. J. Haapola, Z. Shelby, C.P. Raez, P. Mahonen, Cross-layer energy analysis of multi-hop wireless sensor networks, in *EWSN'05* (2005), pp. 33–44
9. I.F. Akyildiz, W. Su, Y. Sankarasubramaniam, E. Cayirci: Wireless sensor networks: a survey. Comput. Netw. **38**(4), 393–422 (2002)
10. B. Son, Y.-S. Her, K. Shim, J.-G. Kim: Development of an automatic people-counting and environment monitoring system based on wireless sensor network in real time; To realize in Korea Mountains, in *Proceedings of International Conference on Multimedia and Ubiquitous Engineering* (2007), pp. 579–584
11. E.M. Petriu, N.D. Georganas, D.C. Petriu, D. Makrakis, V.Z. Groza: Sensor-based information appliances. IEEE Instrum. Meas. Mag. **3**, 31–35 (2000)
12. I.A. Essa: Ubiquitous sensing for smart and aware environments. IEEE Pers. Commun. **7**, 47–49 (2000)
13. N. Noury, T. Herve, V. Rialle, G. Virone, E. Mercier, G. Morey, A. Moro, T. Porcheron: Monitoring behavior in home using a smart fall sensor and position sensors, in *IEEE-EMBS Special Topic Conference on Microtechnologies in Medicine and Biology* (2000), pp. 607–610

14. N. Bulusu, D. Estrin, L. Girod, J. Heidemann: Scalable coordination for wireless sensor networks: self-configuring localization systems, in *International Symposium on Communication Theory and Applications* (2001), pp. 44–48

15. F. Li, G. Yu, X. Yang, C. Li, Z. Feng: A slack factors based real-time query processing approach in wireless sensor networks, in *Seventh International Conference on Web-Age Information Management Workshops* (2006), pp. 3–10

16. E. Shih, S. Cho, N. Ickes, R. Min, A. Sinha, A. Wang, A. Chandrakasan: Physical layer driven protocol and algorithm design for energy-efficient wireless sensor networks, in *Proceedings of the ACM MobiCom* (2001), pp. 272–286

17. I.F. Akyildiz, W. Su, Y. Sankarasubramaniam, E. Cayirci, A survey on sensor networks. IEEE Commun. Mag **40**(8), 102–114 (2002)

18. A. Ganz, Z. Ganz, K. Wongthavarawat, *Multimedia Wireless Networks: Technologies, Standards and QoS* (Prentice Hall Ltd, Publication, 2004)

19. W. Du, D. Navarro, F. Mieyeville, F. Gaffiot, Towards a taxonomy of simulation tools for wireless sensor networks, in *Proceedings of SIMUTools'10: The Third International ICST Conference on Simulation Tools and Techniques* (2010), p. 52

20. NS-2, [Online]. Available: http://www.isi.edu/nsnam/ns/

Chapter 2
LRTHR: Link-Reliability Based Two-Hop Routing for WSNs

Abstract This chapter proposes a Link Reliability based Two-Hop Routing protocol for Wireless Sensor Networks (WSNs). The protocol achieves to reduce packet deadline miss ratio (DMR) while considering link reliability, two-hop delay, and power efficiency and utilizes memory and computational effective methods for estimating the link metrics. Numerical results provide insights that the protocol has a lower packet deadline miss ratio and results in longer sensor network lifetime. The results show that the proposed protocol is a feasible solution to the QoS routing problem in WSNs that support real-time applications.

2.1 Introduction

Emerging WSNs have a set of QoS requirements that include timeliness, high reliability, availability, and integrity. It is often necessary for sensors to communicate in real-time with reliability to meet application constraints. To support such applications, a real-time communication protocol must adapt its behavior based on packet deadlines. Due to resource constraints of WSN platforms, a WSN protocol should introduce minimal overhead in terms of communication and energy consumption. Supporting real-time QoS in WSN can be addressed from different layers and domains. Cross-layer optimization using Medium Access Control (MAC) and network layer routing protocol has the potential for further improvements.

Li et al. [1] propose a two-hop neighborhood information based real-time routing protocol for WSN called Two-Hop Velocity Based Routing (THVR). They adopt the approach of mapping packet deadline to velocity as in SPEED [2]; however, the routing decision is made based on the two-hop velocity. An energy-efficient probabilistic drop is used to save energy while reducing DMR (Deadline Miss Ratio). In case packet deadline requirement is not stringent, a mechanism is embedded that can release the nodes which are frequently chosen as the forwarder. An improvement

---

Reprinted, with permission, from National Institute of Information and Communications Technology (NICT), Proceedings of the 16th International Symposium on Wireless Personal Multimedia Communications (WPMC'13), Copyright 2013. Reprinted by permission from International Journal of Information Processing, vol. 7, no. 1, pp. 15–29, Copyright 2013.

on energy consumption balance throughout the network is achieved. However, the protocols does not consider reliability while deciding the route.

The timeliness and reliability level for data exchanged between sensors and control station is of paramount importance, especially in real time scenarios. The deadline miss ratio (DMR) [3], defined as the ratio of packets that cannot meet the deadlines should be minimized. Sensor nodes typically use batteries for energy supply. Hence, energy efficiency and load balancing form important objectives while designing protocols for WSNs. Therefore, providing corresponding QoS in such scenarios pose to be a great challenge. Our proposed protocol is motivated primarily by the deficiencies of the previous works and aims to provide better Quality of Service with enhanced reliability.

This chapter incorporates QoS parameters in making routing decisions, i.e., (i) reliability (ii) latency, and (iii) energy efficiency. Traffic should be delivered with reliability and within a deadline. Furthermore, energy efficiency is intertwined with the protocol to achieve a longer network lifetime. Hence, the protocol is named, Link Reliability based Two-Hop Routing (LRTHR). The protocol proposes the following features.

(i) Link reliability is considered while choosing the next router; this selects paths that have a higher probability of successful delivery.
(ii) Routing decision is based on two-hop neighborhood information and dynamic velocity that can be modified according to the required deadline, this results in significant reduction in end-to-end DMR (deadline miss ratio).
(iii) Choosing nodes with higher residual energy balances the load among nodes and results in an enhanced lifetime of the network.

The proposed protocol is devised using a modular design; separate modules are dedicated to each QoS requirement. The link reliability estimation and link delay estimation modules use memory and computationally effective methods suitable for WSNs. The node forwarding module is able to make the optimal routing decision using the estimated metrics.

2.2 Related Works

Stateless routing protocols which do not maintain per-route state is a favorable approach for WSNs. The idea of stateless routing is to use location information available to a node locally for routing, i.e., the location of its own and that of its one-hop neighbors without the knowledge about the entire network. These protocols scale well in terms of routing overhead because the tracked routing information does not grow with the network size or the number of active sinks. Parameters like distance to sink, energy efficiency, and data aggregation need to be considered to select the next router among the one-hop neighbors.

Sequential Assignment Routing (SAR) [4] is the first routing protocol for sensor networks that creates a notion of QoS for sensor networks. The protocol creates multiple trees routed from one-hop neighbors of the sink by taking into consideration both energy resources, QoS metric on each path, and priority level of each packet. By using the created trees, multiple paths from the sink to sensors are formed, only one of which is used and the rest are kept as a backup. For each packet routed through the network, a weighted QoS metric is computed as the product of the additive QoS metric and a weight coefficient associated with the priority level of that packet for the purposes of performance evaluation. The objective of the SAR algorithm is to minimize the average weighted QoS metric throughout the lifetime of the network. However, the protocol suffers from the overhead of maintaining the tables and states at each sensor node especially when the number of nodes is large.

SPEED (Stateless Protocol for End-to-End Delay) [2] is a well known stateless routing protocol for real-time communication in sensor networks. It is based on geometric routing protocols such as greedy forwarding GPSR (Greedy Perimeter State Routing) [5, 6]. It uses non-deterministic forwarding to balance each flow among multiple concurrent routes.

The SPEED scheme needs each node to manage information about its neighbors and uses location-based routing to descover paths. SPEED strives to guarantee a definite speed for each packet in the network hence the application making the routing decision can assess the end-to-end delay for the packets by examining the distance to the sink and the speed of the packet. Further, SPEED can implement congestion avoidance when the network is overloaded. The routing module is called Stateless Non-Deterministic Geographic Forwarding (SNGF) works with four other modules at the network layer, as shown in Fig. 2.1.

The beacon exchange module gathers information about the nodes and their location. Delay estimation at each node is basically made by computing the elapsed time when an ACK is received from a neighbor as a response to a transmitted data packet. By checking the delay values, SNGF selects the node that meets the speed requirement. If there is no such node, the relay ratio of the node is checked. The Neighborhood Feedback Loop (NFL) module combines Medium Access Control (MAC) and network layer mechanism and is responsible for calculating the relay ratio by looking at the miss ratios of the neighbors of a node (the nodes which could

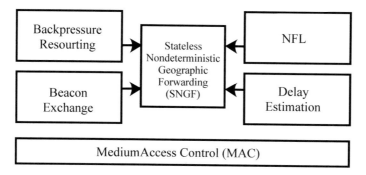

Fig. 2.1 SPEED protocol [2]

not provide the desired speed) and this ratio is fed to the SNGF module. If the relay ratio is below a randomly generated number between 0 and 1, the packet is dropped. Finally, the back pressure rerouting module is utilized to prevent voids when a node fails to find a next-hop node and to clear congestion by sending messages back to the source nodes so that they try to find new routes. However, SPEED does not take any energy metric into account in its routing protocol.

Lu et al. [7] describe a packet scheduling policy called Velocity Monotonic Scheduling, which inherently accounts for both time and distance constraints. MMSPEED (Multi-path and Multi-SPEED Routing Protocol) [8] is an extension of SPEED that focuses on differentiated QoS options for real-time applications with multiple different deadlines. It provides differentiated QoS options both in the timeliness domain and the reliability domain. For timeliness, multiple QoS levels are supported by providing multiple data delivery speed options. For reliability, multiple requirements are supported by probabilistic multi-path forwarding. The protocol provides end-to-end QoS provisioning by employing localized geographic forwarding using immediate neighbor information without end-to-end path discovery and maintenance. It utilizes dynamic compensation for the inaccuracy of local decision as a packet travels towards its destination. The protocol adapts to network dynamics. MMSPEED does not include energy metrics during QoS route selection.

Chipera et al. [9] (RPAR:Real-Time Power Aware Routing) have proposed another variant of SPEED, where a node changes its transmission power by the progress towards the destination and the packet's slack time in order to meet the required velocity; they have not considered residual energy and reliability.

Mahapatra et al. [10] assign an urgency factor to every packet depending on the residual distance and time the packet needs to travel and determines the distance the packet needs to be forwarded closer to the destination to meet its deadline. Multipath routing is performed only at the source node for increasing reliability. Some routing protocols with congestion awareness have been proposed in [11, 12]. Other geographic routing protocols such as [13–16] deal only with energy efficiency and transmission power in determining the next router.

Seada et al. [17] propose the PRR (Packet Reception Rate) × Distance greedy forwarding that selects the next forwarding node by multiplying the PRR by the distance to the destination. Recent geographical routing protocols have been proposed, such as DARA (Distributed Aggregate Routing Algorithm) [18], GREES (Geographic Routing with Environmental Energy Supply) [19], DHGR (Dynamic Hybrid Geographical Routing) [20], and EAGFS (Energy Aware Geographical Forwarding Scheme) [14]. They define either the same combined metric (of all the considered QoS metrics) [2, 14, 19], or several services but with respect to only one metric [8, 9].

Sharif et al. [21] present a new transport layer protocol that prioritizes sensed information based on its nature while simultaneously supporting the data reliability and congestion control features. Rusli et al. [22] proposed an analytical framework model based on Markov Chain of OR and M/D/l/K queue to measure its performance in terms of end-to-end delay and reliability in WSNs.

Koulali et al. [23] propose a hybrid QoS routing protocol for WSNs based on a customized Distributed Genetic Algorithm (DGA) that accounts for delay and energy constraints. Yunbo Wang et al. [24] investigate the end-to-end delay distribution, they develop a comprehensive cross-layer analysis framework, which employs a stochastic queuing model in realistic channel environments. Ehsan et al. [25] propose energy and cross-layer aware routing schemes for multichannel access WSNs that account for radio, MAC contention, and network constraints.

Park et al. [26] present a reliable routing mechanism that provides real-time transfer of important data, they describe a weighted link quality metric that reflects the TX/RX traffic flow to select the reliable route over the routing path. A cross-layer routing protocol is designed in order to reduce the data queue processing time and to send out the priority data at both the network and MAC layer.

Aissani et al. [27] propose an oriented void avoidance scheme guided by the target location with respect to the center of the void. The scheme uses the right-hand rule to discover boundary nodes of the void and geometric formulas to obtain the forwarding region of a sender node located at one-hop near the void. This node reduces its set of forwarding candidate nodes according to its already obtained forwarding region. Park et al. [28] propose an efficient routing scheme that provides real-time transfer of a large amount of image data. Seungmin et al. [29] propose a reliable and real-time service protocol with geographical parallel track concept. The parallel track concept provides the information of each path to all paths and the branch of multi-path occurs only by real-time constraint.

All the above routing protocols are based on one-hop neighborhood information. However, it is expected that multi-hop information can lead to improved performance in many issues including message broadcasting and routing. Tavallaie et al. [30] propose a QoS-aware routing protocol, called Maximum Speed Routing Protocol (MSRP) for WSNs to provide QoS-guarantee in the timeliness domain. MSRP is based on two-hop neighborhood information with low control overhead and it can improve timeliness by sending packets with maximum speed across the network. Also, MSRP considers the distance between a neighbor and destination to determine the next forwarding node and uses a different method to estimate the delay between two neighbors.

Yim et al. [31] present a receiver-based beacon-less routing for real-time services. A novel delay estimation strategy is designed where the single hop delay from a sender to a receiver could be calculated by a receiver but not a sender. Therefore, the receiver itself makes a decision whether the desired time requirement is satisfied. Spohn et al. [32] propose a localized algorithm for computing two-hop connected dominating set to reduce the number of redundant broadcast transmissions. An analysis in [33] shows that in a network of n nodes of a total of $O(n)$ messages are required to obtain two-hop neighborhood information and each message has $O(logn)$ bits.

Chen et al. [34] study the performance of one-hop, two-hop, and three-hop neighborhood information based routing and proposes that the gain from two-hop to three-hop is relatively minimal, while that from one-hop to two-hop based routing is significant. Quang et al. [35] propose gradient routing with two-hop information for industrial wireless sensor networks to enhance real-time performance with energy efficiency. Two-hop information routing is adopted based on the number of hops to the sink instead of distance and an acknowledgment control scheme reduces energy consumption and computational complexity.

Jung et al. [36] propose a novel real-time routing protocol based on reactive and restricted zone search. The proposed protocol minimizes the deadline miss ratio and eliminates the two inefficiencies of a two-hop on demand multi-hop lookahead strategy. Reactive multi-hop neighborhood information obtained is fulfilled only by a small number of sensor nodes within a restricted zone around a data forwarding path from the source to the destination. Diop et al. [37] propose a two-hop neighborhood information-based cover set selection to determine the most relevant cover sets in order to optimize the performance of image transfer from multiple sensor nodes to sink. A multi-path extension of Greedy Perimeter Stateless Routing (called T-GPSR) wherein routing decisions are also based on two-hop neighborhood information is proposed.

Li et al. [1] propose a Two-Hop Velocity Based Routing Protocol (THVR). The routing choice is decided on the two-hop relay velocity and residual energy, an energy-efficient packet drop control is included to enhance packet utilization efficiency while keeping low packet deadline miss ratio. However, THVR does not consider reliability while deciding the route. Shiva Prakash et al. [38] propose a different approach from THVR. They consider reliability and uses dynamic velocity that can be altered for each packet as per the desired deadline. The work considers energy efficiently and balances the load only among nodes estimated to offer the required QoS. The work in this chapter is compared with few selected state of the art papers considering parameters like QoS metrics, estimation methods, and their performance (Table 2.1).

2.3　System Model and Problem Definition

The topology of a Wireless Sensor Network may be described by a graph $G = (N, L)$, where N is the set of nodes and L is the set of links. The objectives are to,

- Minimize the deadline miss ratio (DMR) and improve the end-to-end reliability of the packets.
- Reduce the end-to-end packet delay.
- Improve the energy efficiency (ECPP-Energy Consumed Per Packet) of the network.

In our network model, we assume the following:

- The wireless sensor nodes consist of N sensor nodes and a sink, the sensors are distributed randomly in a field.
- The nodes are aware of their positions through internal global positioning system (GPS), so each sensor has an estimate of its current position.

Table 2.1   Our results and comparison with previous results for QoS routing in Wireless sensor networks

Related work	Protocol name	Considered metric	Estimation method	Performance
Tian He et al. [2]	SPEED (Stateless Protocol for End-to-End Delay)	One-hop delay and residual energy	EWMA (Exponential Weighted Moving Average)	Improves end-to-end delay and provides good response to congestion in the timeliness and reliability domains
E. Felemban et al. [8]	MMSPEED (Multi-path and Multi-SPEED Routing Protocol)	One-hop delay, link reliability and residual energy	EWMA (Exponential Weighted Moving Average)	Provides service differentiation and probabilistic QoS guarantee
Chipera et al. [9]	RPAR (Real-Time Power Aware Routing)	One-hop delay and transmission power	Jacobson Algorithm	Provides real-time routing and dynamic power adaption to achieve application specific communication delays at low energy cost
Y. Li et al. [1]	THVR (Two-Hop Velocity Based Routing Protocol)	Two-hop delay and residual energy	WMEWMA (Window Mean Exponential Weighted Moving Average)	Routing Decision is made based on two-hop velocity integrated with energy balancing mechanism which achieves lower end-to-end DMR and higher energy utilization efficiency
T. Shiva Prakash et al. [38]	LRTHR (Link Reliability based Two-Hop Routing)	Two-hop delay, link reliability and residual energy	EWMA (Exponential Weighted Moving Average) and WMEWMA (Window Mean Exponential Weighted Moving Average)	The protocol considers link reliability and uses dynamic velocity as per the desired deadline, energy is efficiently balanced among the nodes

- The N sensor nodes are powered by a nonrenewable on board energy source. When this energy supply is exhausted the sensor becomes non-operational. All nodes are supposed to be aware of their residual energy and have the same transmission power range.
- The sensors share the same wireless medium, each packet is transmitted as a local broadcast in the neighborhood. The sensors are neighbors if they are in the transmission range of each other and can directly communicate with each other. We assume a MAC protocol, i.e., IEEE 802.11 which ensures that among the neighbors in the local broadcast range, only the intended receiver keeps the packet and the other neighbors discard the packet.
- Like all localization techniques [2, 8, 19, 39, 40] each node needs to be aware of its neighboring nodes current state (ID, position, link reliability, residual energy etc), this is done *via* HELLO messages.
- Nodes are assumed to be stationary or having low mobility, else additional HELLO messages are needed to keep the nodes up-to-date about the neighbor nodes.
- In addition, each node sends a second set of HELLO messages to all its neighbors informing them about its one-hop neighbors. Hence, each node is aware of its one-hop and two-hop neighbors and their current state.
- The network density is assumed to be high enough to prevent the void situation.

2.4 Algorithm

LRTHR has three components: a link reliability estimator, a delay estimator, a node forwarding metric incorporated with the dynamic velocity assignment policy. The proposed LRTHR protocol implements the modules for estimating transmission delay and packet delivery ratios using efficient methods. The packet delay is estimated at the node itself and the packet delivery ratio is estimated by the neighboring nodes. These parameters are updated on the reception of a HELLO packet, the HELLO messages are periodically broadcasted to update the estimation parameters. The overhead caused by the one-hop and two-hop updating is reduced by piggybacking the information in ACK, hence improving the energy efficiency. The notations used in the Algorithm are given in Table 2.2. The protocol is based on the following parameters: (i) Link Reliability Estimation; (ii) Link Delay Estimation; and (iii) Node Forwarding Metric.

2.4.1 Link Reliability Estimation

The Packet Reception Ratio (PRR) of the link relaying node x to y is denoted by prr_{xy}. It denotes the probability of successful delivery over the link. Window Mean Exponential Weighted Moving Average (WMEWMA) based link quality estimation

Table 2.2 Notations: link reliability based two-hop routing

Symbols	Definition
N	Set of Nodes in the WSN
D	Destination Node
S	Source Node
$dist(x, y)$	Distance between a node pair x, y
$N_1(x)$	Set of one-hop Neighbors of node x
$N_2(x)$	Set of two-hop Neighbors of node x
$F_1^{+P}(x)$	Set of node x's one-hop favorable forwarders
$F_2^{+P}(x, y)$	Set of node x's two-hop favorable forwarders
$delay_{xy}$	Estimated hop delay between x and y
t_{req}	Time deadline to reach Destination
V_{req}	Required end-to-end packet delivery Velocity for deadline t_{req}
V_{xy}	Velocity offered by $y \in F_1^{+P}(x)$d
$V_{xy \to z}$	Velocity offered by $y \in F_2^{+P}(x, y)$
S_{req}	Node pairs satisfying $V_{xy \to z} \geq V_{req}$
E_y^0	Initial energy of node y
E_y	Remaining energy of node y
prr_{xy}	Packet Reception Ratio of link relaying node x to node y
α	Tunable weighting coefficient for delay estimation
β	Tunable weighting coefficient for prr estimation
A	PRR (Packet Reception Ratio) weight factor
B	Velocity weight factor
C	Energy weight factor
$rve_{y \to z}$	Reliability, Velocity, and Energy shared metric

is used for the proposed protocol. The window mean exponential weighted moving average estimation applies filtering on PRR, thus providing a metric that resists transient fluctuations of PRR, yet is responsive to major link quality changes. This parameter is updated by node y at each window and inserted into the HELLO message packet for usage by node x in the next window. Equation 2.1 shows the window mean exponential weighted moving average estimation of the link reliability, r is the number of packets received, m is the number of packets missed which is obtained from MAC feedback, and $\alpha \in [0, 1]$ is the history control factor which controls the effect of the previously estimated value on the new one, $\frac{r}{r+m}$ is the newly measured PRR value.

$$prr_{xy} = \alpha \times prr_{xy} + (1 - \alpha) \times \frac{r}{r + m} \qquad (2.1)$$

The PRR estimator is updated at the receiver side for each w (window size) received packets, the computation complexity of this estimator is $O(1)$. The appropriate values for α and w for a stable window mean exponential weighted moving average is $w = 30$ and $\alpha = 0.6$ [41].

2.4.2 Link Delay Estimation

The delay indicates the time spent to send a packet from node x to its neighbor y; it is comprised of the queuing delay ($delay_Q$), contention delay ($delay_C$), and the transmission delay ($delay_T$).

$$delay_{xy} = delay_Q + delay_C + delay_T \qquad (2.2)$$

If t_s is the time the packet is ready for transmission and becomes head of transmission queue, t_{ack} the time of the reception of acknowledgment, BW the network bandwidth, and $sizeof(ACK)$ is the size of the acknowledgment then, $t_{ack} - sizeof(ACK)/BW - t_s$ is the recently estimated delay and $\beta \in [0, 1]$ is the tunable weighting coefficient. Equation 2.3 shows the EWMA (Exponential Weighted Moving Average) update for delay estimation, which has the advantage of being simple and less resource demanding.

$$delay_{xy} = \beta \times delay_{xy} + (1 - \beta) \times (t_{ack} - size\,of(ACK)/BW - t_s) \qquad (2.3)$$

$delay_{xy}$ includes estimation of the time interval from the packet that becomes head of line of x's transmission queue until its reception at node y. This takes into account all delays due to contention, channel sensing, channel reservation (RTS/CTS) if any, depending on the medium access control (MAC) protocol, time slots etc. The computation complexity of this estimator is $O(1)$. The delay information is further exchanged among two-hop neighbors.

2.4.3 Node Forwarding Metric

A wireless sensor network is described by a graph $G = (N, L)$. If node x can transmit a message directly to node y, the ordered pair is an element of L. We define for each node x the set $N_1(x)$, which contains the nodes in the network G that are one-hop, i.e., direct neighbors of x.

$$N_1(x) = \{y : (x; y) \in E \text{ and } y \neq x\} \qquad (2.4)$$

Likewise, the two-hop neighbors of x is the set $N_2(x)$, i.e.,

$$N_2(x) = \{z : (y; z) \in E \text{ and } y \in N_1(x), z \neq x\} \qquad (2.5)$$

Algorithm 2.1: Link Reliability Based Two-Hop Routing (LRTHR)

Input: $x, D, F_1^{+P}(x), F_2^{+P}(x), lt$
Output: Node y providing positive progress towards D

1 $V_{req} = \frac{dist(x,D)}{lt}$;

2 **for** *each* $y \in F_2^{+P}(x)$ **do**

3 $\quad \Big| \quad V_{xy \to z} = \frac{dist(x,D) - dist(k,D)}{delay_{xy} + delay_{yz}}$;

4 $S_{req} = \{F_2^{+P}(x) : V_{xy \to z} \geq V_{req}\}$;

5 **if** $(|S_{req}|) = 1$ **then**

6 $\quad \Big| \quad$ return $y \in S_{req}$;

7 **else**

8 $\quad \Big|$ **for** *each* $y \in S_{req}$ **do**

9 $\quad \Big| \quad \Big| \quad rve_{xy \to z} = A \times \dfrac{prr_{xy}}{\displaystyle\sum_{y \in S_{req}}(prr_{xy})} + B \times \dfrac{V_{xy \to z}}{\displaystyle\sum_{y \in S_{req}} V_{xy \to z}} + C \times \dfrac{E_y/E_y^0}{\displaystyle\sum_{y \in S_{req}}(E_y/E_y^0)}$;

10 $\quad \Big| \quad \Big|$ Find y with $Max\{rve_{xy \to z}\}$;

11 **return** $y \in S_{req}$;

The euclidean distance between a pair of nodes x and y is defined by $dist(x, y)$. We define $F_1^{+P}(x)$ as the set of x's one-hop favorable forwarders providing positive progress towards the destination D. It consists of nodes that are closer to the destination than x, i.e.,

$$F_1^{+P}(x) = \{y \in N_1(x) : dist(x, D) - dist(y, D) > 0\} \qquad (2.6)$$

$F_2^{+P}(x)$ is defined as the set of two-hop favorable forwarders, i.e.,

$$F_2^{+P}(x) = \{y \in F_1^{+P}(x), z \in N_1(y) : dist(y, D) - dist(z, D) > 0\} \qquad (2.7)$$

We define two velocities; the required velocity V_{req} and the velocity offered by the two-hop favorable forwarding pairs. In SPEED, the velocity provided by each of the forwarding nodes in $(F_1^{+P}(x))$ is.

$$V_{xy} = \frac{dist(x, D) - dist(y, D)}{delay_{xy}} \qquad (2.8)$$

As in THVR, by two-hop knowledge, node x can calculate the velocity offered by each of the two-hop favorable forwarding pairs $(F_1^{+P}(x), F_2^{+P}(x))$, i.e.,

$$V_{xy \to z} = \frac{dist(x, D) - dist(z, D)}{delay_{xy} + delay_{yz}} \qquad (2.9)$$

where, $y \in F_1^{+P}(x)$ and $z \in F_2^{+P}(x)$. The required velocity is relative to the progress made towards the destination [9] and the time remaining to the deadline, lt (lag time). The lag time is the time remaining until the packet deadline expires. At each hop, the transmitter renews this parameter in the packet header, i.e.,

$$lt = lt_p - (t_{ttx} - t_{rx} + size\,of\,(packet)/BW) \tag{2.10}$$

where lt is the time remaining to the deadline (t_{req}), lt_p is the previous value of lt, ($t_{ttx} - t_{rx} + sizeof(packet)/BW$) accounts for the delay from reception of the packet until transmission. On reception of the packet the node x, uses lt to calculate the required velocity V_{req} for all nodes in ($F_1^{+P}(x), F_2^{+P}(x)$) as in Eq. 2.11.

$$V_{req} = \frac{dist(x, D)}{lt} \tag{2.11}$$

The node pairs satisfying $V_{xy \to z} \geq V_{req}$ form the set of nodes S_{req}. For the set S_{req} we calculate the shared metric ($rve_{xy \to z}$), incorporating the node's link reliability, velocity towards destination, and remaining energy level of neighbors in S_{req} as depicted in Eq. 2.12.

$$rve_{xy \to z} = A \times \frac{prr_{xy}}{\displaystyle\sum_{y \in S_{req}} (prr_{xy})} + B \times \frac{V_{xy \to z}}{\displaystyle\sum_{y \in S_{req}} V_{xy \to z}} + C \times \frac{E_y/E_y^0}{\displaystyle\sum_{y \in S_{req}} (E_y/E_y^0)} \tag{2.12}$$

A, B, and C are the weighting factors for combining reliability, velocity, and energy into the shared metric ($A + B + C = 1$). The node y with the largest $rve_{xy \to z}$ is chosen as the forwarder and the process is continuous till the destination is reached. The Link Reliability Based Two-Hop Routing is given in Algorithm 2.1, the computation complexity of this algorithm is $O(F_2^{+P}(x))$. The proposed protocol is different from THVR, as it considers reliability and dynamic velocity that can be adjusted for each packet according to the required deadline. It balances the load only among nodes estimated to offer the required QoS.

2.4.4   LRTHR: An Example

We illustrate the proposed protocol in a case study. It is observed from Fig. 2.2 that if a packet is to be sent from S to D, then nodes 1, 2, 3, 4 $\in F_1^{+P}(S)$, 5,6 $\in F_1^{+P}(1)$, 7 $\in F_1^{+P}(2)$, 10 $\in F_1^{+P}(4)$, 14 $\in F_1^{+P}(8)$, 12,13 $\in F_1^{+P}(7)$, 7 $\in F_1^{+P}(2)$.

The distance between the various nodes and the destination are (S, D) = 150 m, (1, D) = 120 m, (2, D) = 108 m, (3, D) = 114 m, (4, D) = 127.5 m (5, D) = 117 m, (6, D) = 97.5 m, (7, D) = 110 m, (8, D) = 90 m, (9, D) = 97.5 m and (10, D) = 117 m. Let the required velocity

Fig. 2.2 Illustration of the
working of LRTHR protocol

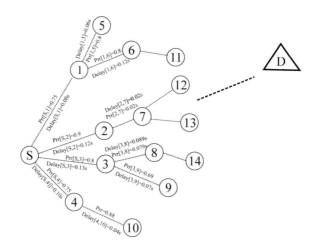

$$V_{req} = \frac{150m}{0.55s} = 272.7m/s$$

Here, the end-to-end deadline is 0.55s. By Eq. 2.8, each node calculates the velocity
(V_{xy}) provided by each of its forwarding nodes in $F_1^{+p}(S)$,

$$V_{S1} = \frac{150m - 120m}{0.08s} = 375m/s$$

Likewise, the velocity provided by $V_{S2} = (150m - 108m)/0.12s = 350m/s$, $V_{S3} = (150m - 114m)/0.13s = 276.92m/s$ and $V_{S4} = (150m - 127.5m)/0.10s = 225m/s$. Thus, from SPEED node 1 has the largest velocity greater than V_{req} and is
chosen as the forwarder and so on.

As per THVR, node S will search among its two-hop neighbors $F_2^{+p}(S)$, i.e.,
nodes (5, 6, 7, 8, 9, 10) and calculate the velocity ($V_{xy \rightarrow z}$) provided by each of the
two-hop pairs by Eq. 2.9,

$$V_{S3 \rightarrow 8} = \frac{dist(S, D) - dist(8, D)}{delay_{S3} + delay_{38}}$$
$$= \frac{150m - 90m}{0.13s + 0.079s}$$
$$= 287.08m/s$$

Similarly, the velocity provided by the two-hop pairs

$$V_{S1 \rightarrow 5} = (150m - 117m)/(0.11s + 0.06s) = 235.7m/s$$
$$V_{S1 \rightarrow 6} = (150m - 97.5m)/(0.08s + 0.12s) = 262.5m/s$$
$$V_{S2 \rightarrow 7} = (150m - 110m)/(0.12s + 0.02s) = 285.7m/s$$

$$V_{S3 \to 9} = (150m - 97.5m)/(0.13s + 0.07s) = 262.5m/s$$
$$V_{S4 \to 10} = (150m - 117m)/(0.10s + 0.04s) = 235.7m/s$$

The velocity provided by $V_{S3 \to 8}$ is greater than V_{req} and is also the largest among the other two-hop pairs shown above. Therefore, node 3 will be chosen as the immediate forwarder. But, by LRTHR we also consider the PRR of the links while choosing the next forwarder, the PRR of link to node 2 is 0.9 and that to link 3 is 0.85, hence node 2 is chosen as the next hop candidate. If the packet arriving at node 2 has taken 0.13 ms to travel, then the new deadline to reach the destination is 0.42 s. The required velocity is updated at node 2 and the next forwarder is chosen based on this new value.

In LRTHR, by selecting a link that provides higher PRR, the protocol aids in increasing the probability of successful packet delivery to the forwarding node. In THVR, if a path from source to destination has a link with a poor packet reception ratio, then this may increase the DMR. By, selecting links providing greater PRR on the route, the throughput (amount of traffic successfully received by the destination) can be increased, results in a lower DMR and augments energy efficiency of the forwarding nodes due to lower number of collisions and re-transmissions. Also, the two-hop neighborhood information incorporated with the dynamic velocity assignment policy provides enhanced foresight to the sender in identifying the node pair that can provide the largest velocity towards the destination.

2.5 Performance Evaluation

To evaluate the proposed protocol, we carried out a simulation study using *ns*-2 [42]. The proposed protocol (LRTHR) is compared with THVR and SPEED. The simulation configuration consists of 200 nodes located in a 200 m^2 area. Nodes are distributed following Poisson point process with a node density of 0.005 node/m^2. The source nodes are located in the region (40m, 40m) while the sink is placed around the area (200m, 200m). The source generated a CBR flow of 1 packet/second with a packet size of 150 bytes.

The MAC layer, link quality, and energy consumption parameters are set as per Mica2 Motes [43] with MPR400 radio as per THVR. Table 2.3 summarizes the simulation parameters. THVR and SPEED are QoS protocols and a comparison of DMR (Deadline Miss Ratio), ECPP (Energy Consumed Per Packet, i.e., the total energy expended divided by the number of packets effectively transmitted), the packet average delay (mean of packet delay) and worst-case delay (largest value sustained by the successfully transmitted packet) are obtained and shown in the graphs below.

In the first set of simulations, we consider 10 source nodes with varying deadlines from 100 to 700 ms. In THVR, the weighting factor C is set at 0.9 to favor lower end-to-end delay performance, likewise in SPEED we assign K = 10 for shorter

Table 2.3 Simulation parameters

Simulation parameters	Value
Number of nodes	200
Simulation topology	200m × 200m
Traffic	CBR
Payload size	150 Bytes
Transmission range	40m
Initial battery energy	2.0 Joules
Energy consumed during transmit	0.0255 Joule
Energy consumed during receive	0.021 Joule
Energy consumed during sleep	0.000005 Joule
Energy consumed during idle	0.0096 Joule
MAC layer	802.11 with DCF
Propagation model	Free space
Hello period	5 s
PRR—WMEWMA window	30
PRR—WMEWMA weight factor (α)	0.6
Delay—EWMA weight factor (β)	0.5

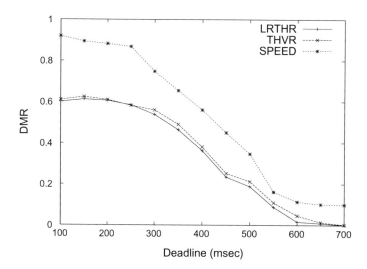

Fig. 2.3 DMR versus deadline

end-to-end delay. In the proposed protocol we set weighting factors (A, B, C) at (0.1, 0.8, 0.1). In each run, 500 packets are transmitted.

Figure 2.3 illustrates the efficiency of the LRTHR algorithm in reducing the DMR; the DMR characteristics of LRTHR and THVR are similar untill a delay of 250 ms and the performance of LRTHR is better than THVR by 10% for all other deadlines.

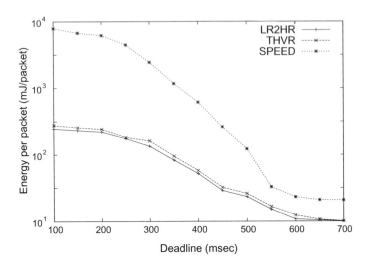

Fig. 2.4 ECPP versus deadline

As the deadline increases, the DMRs eventually converge to zero at about 675 ms. In comparison, as shown in Fig. 2.3 THVR has a higher DMR, the initiative drop control has a slightly negative effect on the DMR.

In SPEED, when the deadline is stringent (less than 300 ms), the SPEED protocol drops packets aggressively at lower deadlines, resulting in an overall higher DMR. Even, when the deadline is 700 ms the DMR has not yet converged to zero. The two-hop based routing and the dynamic velocity of the LRTHR algorithm is able to aggressively route more packets within the deadline to the sink node, also the protocol is able to select the reliable paths between the sources and the sink, hence it is observed that LRTHR has a lower DMR than the other algorithms.

As depicted in Fig. 2.4, the energy consumption per packet (ECPP) successfully transmitted decreases as the deadline increases. The energy consumption has a similar tendency in both LRTHR and THVR but SPEED has a higher energy utilization. The slight variation of the LRTHR protocol is due to the link reliability incorporated in the route selection which may sometimes select a longer path to the destination resulting in higher energy utilization on some paths, but the dynamic velocity minimizes this effect. By, selecting links providing higher PRR on the route to the sink, the energy consumption of the forwarding nodes can be minimized, due to lower number of collisions and re-transmissions. In addition, in the proposed protocol, the link delay and packet delivery ratios are updated by piggybacking the information in ACK and helps in reducing the number of feedback packets and reducing the total energy consumed.

In THVR, the initiative drop control module drops the packet if it is near the source and cannot meet the required velocity from the perspective of energy utilization. But in our proposed protocol, the packet is not dropped since the dynamic velocity approach aids in ensuring that the packet eventually meets the deadline and more

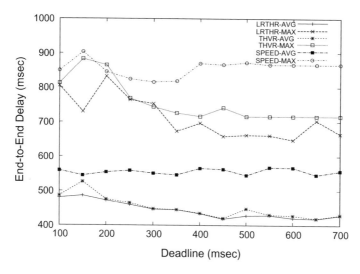

Fig. 2.5 Average and worst case delay versus deadline

packets are forwarded to the destination and improves the ECPP. Generally, LRTHR has a lower energy consumption level compared to the other protocols.

Figure 2.5 compares the packet end-to-end average and worst-case delays, respectively. It is observed that THVR and LRTHR protocols have similar performance in the average end-to-end delay. The performance of LRTHR is better when the algorithms are compared in the worst-case delays. The performance of SPEED is poor in both the average and worst-case delays. In LRTHR, paths from source to sink are shorter due to the dynamic velocity, two-hop information and variation in the delays because of link reliability, THVR selects path based only on two-hop routing information.

Additionally, we examine the performance of the protocols under different loads. The number of sources is increased from 6 to 13, while the deadline requirement is fixed at 350 ms. Each source generates a CBR flow of 1 packet/second with a packet size of 150 bytes.

In Figs. 2.6 and 2.7, it is observed that the DMR and ECPP plots ascend as the number of sources increase. The increase is resulted by the elevated channel busy probability, packet contentions at MAC and network congestion by the increased number of sources and resulting traffic. It is observed from Figs. 2.6 and 2.7 that LRTHR protocol has lower DMR and also lower energy consumption per successfully transmitted packet.

Figure 2.8 shows the packet end-to-end average and worst-case delays, respectively. It is observed that all the three protocols have similar performance in the average and worst-case end-to-end delay, untill the number of sources is 10. The performance of LRTHR is better because the algorithm is able to spread the routes

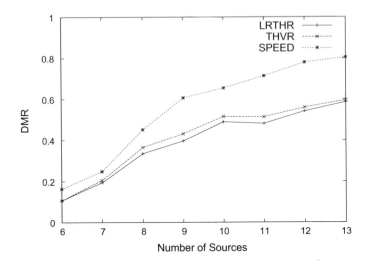

Fig. 2.6 DMR versus number of sources

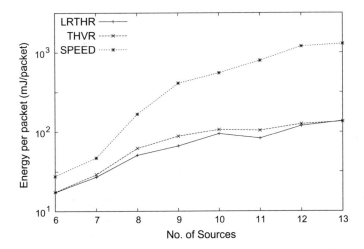

Fig. 2.7 ECPP versus number of sources

to the destination, since greater number of source nodes help in finding links with more reliable alternate paths and in addition provides better energy utilization.

Finally, we study the performance of the residual energy cost function, the packet deadline is relaxed to a large value. Hence, when many nodes can provide the required velocity, a node that has high residual energy is chosen as a forwarding node. This results in uniform load balancing among the nodes of the network.

There are totally 200 nodes including 4 source nodes. The deadline is set to a large value of 600 ms. In THVR, the weighting factor C is set at 0.7 to have a larger weighting on residual energy. In the proposed protocol, we set weighting factors

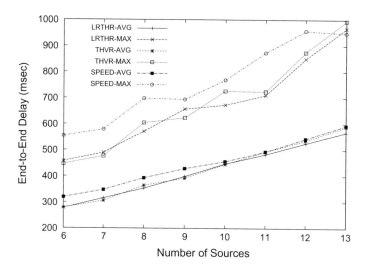

Fig. 2.8 Average and worst case delay versus number of sources

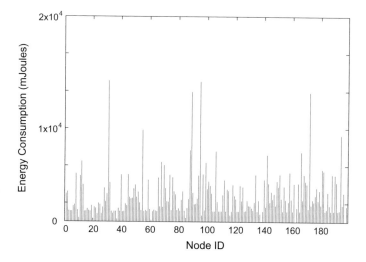

Fig. 2.9 Node energy consumption in THVR

(A, B, C) to (0.1, 0.7, 0.2). Figures 2.9 and 2.10 show the node energy consumption distribution in THVR and LRTHR, respectively, after 200 runs.

As observed in THVR, some nodes along the path from sources to sink are frequently chosen as forwarders and consume much more energy than the other, while in LRTHR only nodes close to the sources and sink consume relatively high energy. The latter is normal and inevitable especially as there may not be many optimal forwarding options near the sources and sink. Besides, by comparing Figs. 2.9 to 2.10, energy consumption in LRTHR is more evenly distributed among those between

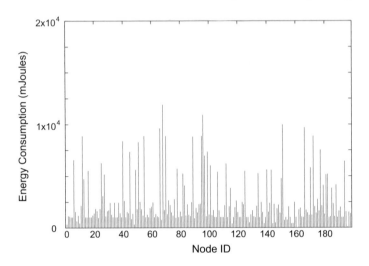

Fig. 2.10 Node energy consumption in LRTHR

source and sink. The link reliability cost function further aids to spread the routes to the destination in comparison to THVR. It is observed that LRTHR has a longer system lifetime due to load balancing.

2.6 Summary

This chapter proposes a link reliability based two-hop neighborhood based Quality of Service (QoS) routing protocol for WSNs. The proposed LRTHR protocol considers reliability and dynamic velocity that can be adjusted for each packet according to the required deadline. It balances the load only among nodes estimated to offer the required QoS. The LRTHR protocol is able to augment real-time delivery by an able integration of link reliability, two-hop information, and dynamic velocity.

References

1. Y. Li, C.S. Chen, Y.-Q. Song, Enhancing real-time delivery in wireless sensor networks with two-hop information. IEEE Trans. Ind. Inform. **5**(2), 113–122 (2009)
2. T. He, J.A. Stankovic, L. Chenyang, T.F. Abdelzaher, A spatiotemporal protocol for wireless sensor network. IEEE Trans. Parallel Distrib. Syst. **16**(10), 995–1006 (2005)
3. J. Stankovic, T. Abdelzaher, C. Lu, L. Sha, J. Hou, Real-time communication and coordination in embedded sensor networks. Proc. IEEE **91**, 1002–1022 (2003)
4. K. Sohrabi, J. Pottie, Protocols for self-organization of wireless sensor network. IEEE Pers. Commun. **7**(5), 16–27 (2000)

5. B. Karp, H.T. Kung, GPSR: greedy perimeter stateless routing for wireless networks, in *Proceedings of the 6th Annual International Conference on Mobile Computing and Networking (MobiCom)* (2000), pp. 243–254

6. P. Bose, P. Morin, I. Stojmenovi, J. Urrutia, Routing with Guaranteed Delivery in Ad hoc Wireless Networks, in *Proceedings of the 3rd ACM International Workshop on Discrete Algorithms and Methods for Mobile Computing and Communications DIALM'99* (1999), pp. 48–55 (Aug 1999)

7. C. Lu, B.M. Blum, T.F. Abdelzaher, J.A. Stankovic, T. He, RAP: a real-time communication architecture for large-scale wireless sensor networks, in *Proceedings ot the IEEE RTAS* (2002)

8. E. Felemban, C.G. Lee, E. Ekici, MMSPEED: multipath multi-speed protocol for QoS guarantee of reliability and timeliness in wireless sensor network. IEEE Trans. Mob. Comput. **5**(6), 738–754 (2006)

9. O. Chipara, Z. He, G. Xing, Q. Chen, X. Wang, C. Lu, J. Stankovic, T. Abdelzaher, Real-time power-aware routing in sensor network, in *Proceedings of the IWQoS* (2006), pp. 83–92

10. A. Mahapatra, K. Anand, D.P. Agrawal, QoS and energy aware routing for real-time traffic in wireless sensor networks. Comput. Commun. **29**(4), 437–445 (2008)

11. D. Tran, H. Raghavendra, Routing with congestion awareness and adaptivity in mobile ad hoc networks, in *Proceedings of the IEEE WCNC* (2005)

12. Y. Sankarasubramaniam, B. Akan, and I. F. Akyildiz: ESRT:Event-to-Sink Reliable Transport in Wireless Sensor Networks, in *Proceedings of the ACM Mobihoc* (2003), pp. 177–188

13. X. Wu, B.J. d"Auriol, J. Cho, S. Lee, Optimal routing in sensor networks for in-home health monitoring with multi factor considerations, In *Proceedings of the Sixth Annual IEEE International Conference on Pervasive Computing and Communication (PERCOM 2008)* (2008), pp. 720–725

14. T.L. Lim, M. Gurusamy, Energy aware geographical routing and topology control to improve network lifetime in wireless sensor networks, in *Proceedings of the IEEE International Conference on Broadband Networks (BROADNETS 05)* (2005) pp. 829–831

15. S. Wu, K.S. Candan, Power Aware Single and Multipath Geographic Routing in Sensor Networks, in *Proceedings of the IEEE International Conference on Broadband Networks (BROADNETS 05)* **5**(7) (2007), pp. 974–997

16. C.-p. Li, W.-j. Hsu, B. Krishnamachari, A. Helmy, A local metric for geographic routing with power control in wireless networks, in *Proceedings of the Second Ann IEEE Conference Sensor and Ad Hoc Communications and Networks (SECON)* (2005), pp. 229–239

17. K. Seada, M. Zuniga, A. Helmy, B. Krishnamachari, Energy efficient forwarding strategies for geographic routing in lossy wireless sensor networks, in *Proceedings of the ACM Sensor Systems* (2004), pp. 108–121

18. M.A. Razzaque, M.M. Alam, C.S. Hong, Multi-constrained QoS geographic routing for heterogeneous traffic in sensor networks. IEICE Trans. Commun. **91B**(8), 2589–2601 (2008)

19. K. Zeng, K. Ren, W. Lou, P.J. Moran, Energy aware efficient geographic routing in lossy wireless sensor networks with environmental energy supply. Wirel. Netw. **15**(1), 39–51 (2009)

20. M. Chen, V. Leung, S. Mao, Y. Xiao, I. Chlamtac, Hybrid geographical routing for flexible energy-delay trade-offs. IEEE Trans. Veh. Technol. **58**(9), 4976–4988 (2009)

21. A. Sharif, V. Potdar, A.J.D Rathnayaka, Prioritizing information for achieving QoS control in WSN, in *Proceedings of the IEEE International Conference on Advanced Information Networking and Applications* (2010), pp. 835–842

22. M.E Rusli, R. Harris, A. Punchihewa, Markov chain-based analytical model of opportunistic routing protocol for wireless sensor networks, in *Proceedings TENCON IEEE Region 10 Conference* (2010), pp. 257–262

23. M. Koulali, A. Kobbane, M. El Koutbi, M. Azizi, QDGRP: a hybrid qos distributed genetic routing protocol for wireless sensor networks, in *Proceedings of the International Conference on Multimedia Computing and Systems* (2012), pp. 47–52

24. Y. Wang, M.C Vuran, S. Goddard: Cross-layer analysis of the end-to-end delay distribution in wireless sensor networks. IEEE Trans. Netw. **20**(1), 305–318 (2012)

25. S. Ehsan, B. Hamdaoui, M. Guizani, Radio and medium access contention aware routing for lifetime maximization in multichannel sensor networks. IEEE Trans. Wirel. Commun. **11**(9), 3058–3067 (2012)
26. H. Park, Z.H. Mir, N.-S. Kim, C.-S. Pyo, Data traffic based route selection for real-time data delivery in wireless sensor networks, in *Proceedings of the IEEE International Conference on Networked Embedded Systems for Enterprise Applications (NESEA)* (2010), pp. 1–5
27. M. Aissani, A. Mellouk, N. Badache, B. Saidani, Oriented void avoidance scheme for real-time routing protocols in wireless sensor networks, in *Proceedings of the IEEE GLOBECOM* (2008), pp. 1–5
28. H. Park, Y.-H. Ham, S.-J. Park, J.-M. Woo, J.-B. Lee, Large data transport for real-time services in sensor networks, in *Proceedings of the Computation World: Future Computing, Service Computation, Cognitive, Adaptive, Content, Patterns* (2009), pp. 404–408
29. S. Oh, Y. Yim, J. Lee, H. Park, S.-H. Kim, A reliable communication strategy for real-time data dissemination in wireless sensor networks, in *Proceedings of the IEEE 26th International Conference on Advanced Information Networking and Applications* (2012), pp. 817–823
30. O. Tavallaie, H.R. Naji, M. Sabaei, N. Arastouie, Providing QoS Guarantee of Timeliness in Wireless Sensor Networks with a New Routing Methodology, in *Proceedings Sixth International Symposium on Telecommunications (IST)* (2012), pp. 674–679
31. Y. Yim, H. Park, J. Lee, S. Oh, S.-H. Kim, Distributed forwarder selection for beaconless real-time routing in wireless sensor networks, in *Proceedings of the IEEE 77th Vehicular Technology Conference (VTC Spring)* (2013), pp. 1–5
32. M. A. Spohn, J. J. Garcia-Luna-Aceves, Enhancing broadcast operations in ad hoc networks with two-hop connected dominating sets, in *Proceedings of the IEEE MASS* (2004), pp. 543–545
33. G. Calinescu, Computing 2-hop neighborhoods in ad hoc wireless networks, in *Proceedings of the Ad Hoc Now* (2003), pp. 175–186
34. C.S. Chen, Y. Li, Y.-Q. Song, An exploration of geographic routing with k-hop based searching in wireless sensor networks, in *Proceedings of the CHINACOM* (2008), pp. 376–381 (2008)
35. P.T.A. Quang, D.-S. Kim, Enhancing real-time delivery of gradient routing for industrial wireless sensor networks. IEEE Trans. Onindustrial Inform. **8**(1), 61–68 (2012)
36. J. Jung, S. Park, E. Lee, S. Oh, S.-H. Kim, Real-time data dissemination based on reactive and restricted zone search in sensor networks, in *Proceedings IEEE 24th International Conference on Advanced Information Networking and Applications* (2010), pp. 925–932
37. M. Diop, C. Pham, O. Thiare, 2-hop neighborhood information for cover set selection in mission-critical surveillance with wireless image sensor networks, in *Proceedings of the Wireless Days (WD)* (2013), pp. 1–7
38. P.T. Shiva, K.B. Raja, K.R. Venugopal, S.S. Iyengar, L.M. Patnaik, Link-reliability based two-hop routing for QoS guarantee in wireless sensor networks, in *IEEE Proceedings of the 16th International Symposium on Wireless Personal Multimedia Communications (WPMC13)* (2013), pp. 1–6
39. T. He, C. Huang, B.M. Blum, J.A. Stankovic, T.F. Abdelzaher, Range-free localization and its impact on large scale sensor networks. ACM Trans. Embed. Comput. Syst. **4**(4), 877–906 (2000)
40. T. Roosta, M. Menzo, S. Sastry, Probabilistic geographical routing protocol for ad-hoc and sensor networks, in *Proceedings of the International Workshop Wireless Ad-Hoc Networks (IWWAN)* (2005)
41. A. Woo, D.E. Culler, Evaluation of efficient link reliability estimators for low-power wireless networks. Technical report, University of California (2003)
42. NS-2, http://www.isi.edu/nsnam/ns/
43. Crossbow Motes, http://www.xbow.com

Chapter 3
FTQAC: Fault Tolerant QoS Adaptive Clustering for WSNs

Abstract This chapter presents and examines an Energy Efficient Fault Tolerant QoS Adaptive Clustering Algorithm (FTQAC) for Wireless Sensor Networks that can support real time traffic. The protocol delivers fault tolerance and energy efficiency by means of a dual cluster head scheme and guarantees the desired QoS by considering delay and bandwidth parameters in the route selection process. Results show that FTQAC decreases overall power utilization and augments network lifetime while sustaining required QoS.

3.1 Introduction

In order to satisfy the QoS requirements and energy constraints for WSNs, hierarchical (clustering) techniques have been an attractive approach to organize sensor networks based on their power levels and proximity. In each cluster, sensor nodes are delegated different roles, such as cluster head or ordinary member node. A cluster head (CH) is elected in each cluster that collects sensed data from member nodes, aggregates and transmits the aggregated data to the next cluster head or to the base station (BS). The role of ordinary member node is to sense data from the environment and communicate the data to the cluster head as shown in Fig. 3.1.

The QBCDCP protocol [1] achieves QoS routing in Wireless Sensor Networks by using delay, along with the transmission energy, as the routing metric while ensuring that bandwidth requirements and end-to-end delay objectives of the application are met in the route selection process. The protocol achieves energy efficiency through a rotating cluster head mechanism and delegation of energy intensive tasks to a single high power Base Station. The QBCDCP scheme shows an increase in sensing node lifetime with the number of clusters, but with a corresponding increase in end-to-end delay.

The cluster based network model provides inherent optimization capabilities at cluster heads, such as data fusion and reduces communication interference by using

Reprinted by permission from Springer Nature: Springer LNEE-7818, Shiva Prakash T., Raja K. B., Venugopal K. R., S. S. Iyengar, L. M. Patnaik, Fault Tolerant QoS Adaptive Clustering for Wireless Sensor Networks, WCSN'13, Copyright (2013).

© Springer Nature Singapore Pte Ltd. 2020
K. R. Venugopal et al., *QoS Routing Algorithms for Wireless Sensor Networks*,
https://doi.org/10.1007/978-981-15-2720-3_3

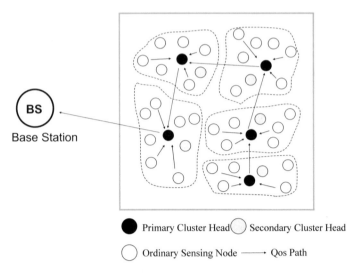

Fig. 3.1 System model

TDMA (Time Division Multiple Access). High energy nodes can be used to process and send the information while low energy nodes can be used to perform the sensing task. Overall, clustering is an excellent approach for achieving scalability, lifetime, energy efficiency, and reduce network contention. While earlier works were primarily focused on the above mentioned aspects, more recent research has begun to consider fault tolerance, reliability, and Quality of Service and our proposed protocol is motivated by these metrics.

The proposed algorithm Fault Tolerant QoS Adaptive Clustering (FTQAC) employs a fault tolerant dual cluster head mechanism in the cluster with respect to the working of the cluster head and guarantees the desired QoS by including delay and bandwidth parameters in the route selection process. Furthermore, the protocol evenly distributes the energy consumption to all nodes so as to extend the sensor network lifetime.

3.2 Related Works

In this section a summary of the current state-of-the-art in hierarchical routing protocols for WSNs are presented with the highlights of the performance issues and limitations of each strategy.

A self-organizing, adaptive clustering scheme that uses randomized rotation of cluster heads to uniformly distribute the energy load among the sensor nodes in the network is proposed in Low-Energy Adaptive Clustering Hierarchy (LEACH) [2]. The cluster heads have the responsibility of collecting data from their clusters and fuse the collected data, hence reducing the number of messages to be sent to the Base Station, which results in lower energy consumption. The broadcast messages, as well as cluster formation messages are transmitted using CSMA (Carrier Sense Multiple Access) to lower collisions. After cluster formation, cluster heads creates a transmission schedule and broadcasts it to all the nodes in their respective cluster. This schedule contains TDMA slots for each neighboring node. This scheduling scheme helps energy minimization at nodes that can power off their radio during all but their scheduled time slot. In the centralized variant of this protocol, LEACH-C [3], the base station manages the clustering procedure.

Despite these benefits, LEACH and LEACH-C suffer several shortcomings. Cluster head selection that uses probability does not naturally lead to minimum energy consumption. Cluster head route messages to the Base Station in a single hop and when the network size grows, it is possible that these cluster heads discharge faster than others and if the distance is large, the messages may not reach the Base Station.

Threshold sensitive Energy Efficient sensor Network (TEEN) [4] and its adaptive version (AdaPtive) Threshold sensitive Energy Efficient sensor Network (APTEEN) [5] are clustering protocols that are similar to LEACH; they are receptive to quick changes in WSNs. The two protocols nominate the transmitting nodes by using threshold schemes. The deficiency of the two schemes are the overhead related to forming of clusters at multiple levels and the process of executing threshold based methods.

Lindsey and Ragavendra propose an efficient chain-based scheme called Power Efficient Gathering in Sensor Information Systems (PEGASIS) [6]. Instead of classifying nodes into clusters, the scheme makes a chain of sensor nodes. As per this structure, each node transmits to and receives from only the nearest nodes of its neighbors. The node carrying out data aggregation transmits the data to the node that communicates with the sink. Every round, a greedy scheme is run to designate one node in the chain to transmit with the sink. The shortcoming of the protocol is that the single leader can itself become a congestion point in the network.

Younis et al. [7] presented a new clustering model called HEED (Hybrid Energy-Efficient Distributed clustering), in which cluster heads are elected through finite iteration, taking into account nodal residual energy and the inner clusters communication costs. The quality of clustering in HEED is better than LEACH, but requires higher communication costs, and the time synchronization difference is relatively large.

Stable Election Protocol [8] utilize non-homogeneous sensor nodes to dispense power uniformly in WSNs. The scheme of cluster head election is based on two distinct levels of power. A node with the maximum weight as per their different power levels is elected as cluster head. Successive cluster heads are selected using this scheme. This ensures that cluster heads are randomly elected and power consumption is evenly distributed among nodes.

Two-Level Hierarchy LEACH (TL-LEACH) [9] protocol selects two sensor nodes in individual cluster as cluster heads; one node acts as the primary cluster head and the other the secondary cluster head. Primary and secondary cluster heads can communicate with each other and secondary cluster heads communicate with nodes in their sub-clusters. The two-level scheme of TL-LEACH lowers the amount of nodes that require to transmit to the base station, efficaciously lowering the total power usage. However, there is a huge probability of rise in overhead at the time of selection of primary and secondary cluster heads which causes higher power consumption.

Chen et al. [10] propose a native unified scheme for selecting a dual cluster head and developed a parameter to quantify QoS in applications of WSNs. The scheme can strengthen the reliability and dependability of WSN by allotting evenly the communication and data fusion load amid the cluster heads. The dual cluster head model can also enhance the life of Wireless Sensor Networks. The drawbacks of the protocol are that the secondary cluster is formed only if the number of nodes in a given cluster is larger than a threshold, the protocol proposed in this chapter always creates a secondary cluster to achieve fault tolerance in WSNs.

Muruganathan et al. [11] propose a Base-Station Controlled Dynamic Clustering Protocol (BCDCP), which employs the high-energy base station to execute most power-hungry tasks and assigns the power evenly among all sensor nodes to augment network lifetime and average power savings. BCDCP relies on the base station to perform balanced cluster formation, path selection, and other energy intensive tasks. Multi-hop communication among cluster heads is employed to reach the base station, through the lowest energy path.

Haiping and Ruchuan [12] propose an innovative clustered control scheme based on location data, priority of coverage, power, and multi-layered architecture. This scheme elects a cluster head as per the geographical locations and residual power at the nodes and assures greater coverage rate for the cluster head by a priority system to evade the dense and sparse distribution of cluster heads. This scheme lowers the power cost by expanding the size of sleeping nodes amid non-media data transmission phase and including many intermediate nodes to forward data during multimedia data transmission which enhance the lifetime of the network.

Ji et al. [13] proposed a protocol that targets on boosting the power efficiency and other QoS metrics by omitting the node with an inaccurate geographic position to be the cluster heads. Feng et al. [14] modeled a High Available Sensor network protocol for Differentiated Services, which calculate the routing gradient with different parameters, and then build two types of routing gradient table for best-effort and real-time service.

EkbataniFard et al. [15] utilized cluster heads as higher energy relay nodes in a two-tiered WSN and these relay nodes create a network among themselves to route data to the sink and implement power efficient QoS routing in cluster based WSNs. Ben-othman et al. [16] proposed an algorithm that implements Quality of Service (QoS) by using a queuing scheme to categorize the traffic into four different queues as per speed. Higher priority queues have outright special advantage over low priority queues.

Aslam et al. [17] presented a mathematical model using Network Calculus for TDMA-based medium access control scheme, where a cluster based system is designed and arrival to service graph is presented. The protocol is used to find the largest delay and backlog limits for applications with QoS needs.

Melodia et al. [18] proposed a novel cross-layer communication model based on the time-hopping impulse radio ultra wide band technology built for flexibly and reliably bringing QoS to heterogeneous applications in WMSNs, by using and regulating interactions among different layers of the protocol stack as per applications needs. Noori et al. [19] proposed a probabilistic scheme for evaluating the network lifetime when actions occur randomly over the network area. A scheme of the packet transmission rate of the sensors is proposed making use of Voronoi tessellation. The probability of accomplishing a given life span by individual sensors is determined and is then utilized to examine the cluster life span. The study combines the result of dynamic cluster head assignment, power model, random deployment of sensors, data compression and packet generation model at the sensors.

Yao et al. [20] propose a novel model which can capture both the factors of energy efficiency and QoS guarantee especially the source-to-sink delay and data-loss probability. Quang and Kim et al. [21] propound a clustering scheme to enhance the performance of the fixed wireless sensor, a multi-level hierarchical structure can be used to reduce the power consumption. In addition to the cluster head, some nodes can be selected as intermediate nodes, each of which manages a sub-cluster, according to their positions. Intermediate nodes aggregate data from general nodes and send them to the cluster head. The selection of intermediate nodes to optimize energy consumption is modeled as a mixed-integer linear programming having high computational complexity; consequently, the lowest energy path searching algorithm is proposed to shorten the computational time.

Chen et al. [22] proposed a robust fault-tolerant Quality of Service (QoS) algorithm, here the aim to attain application QoS demands while increasing the life of the sensors using a hop-by-hop data delivery employing source and path overabundance.

Fapojuwo et al. [1] proposed a Quality of service augmented Base station Controlled Dynamic Clustering Protocol (QBCDCP). The scheme obtains power efficiency through a revolving head clustering mechanism and assignment of power-hungry tasks to a single base station, QoS support parameters like delay and bandwidth are used for the route selection process. Prakash et al. [23] propose a dual cluster head scheme to obtain the fault tolerance and enhance the life of the WSNs, additionally the dual cluster head scheme reduces the end-to-end delay and augments packet delivery ratio (PDR).

3.3 System Model and Problem Definition

In our system model, we assume the following:

- The Wireless Sensor Network consists of N homogeneous sensor nodes, deployed at random locations in a sensor field. An example scenario is shown in Fig. 3.1 where the sensor field is a square area at a distance d_{BS} from a single fixed base-station. The sensors are grouped into one-hop clusters with a specific clustering algorithm. All sensor nodes are immobile.

- All the nodes in the network start with the same initial energy and have limitations with respect to battery, processing, and memory space.
- The N sensor nodes are powered by a nonrenewable on board energy source. When this energy supply is exhausted, the sensor becomes non-operational. All nodes are supposed to be aware of their residual energy and are capable of measuring the signal strength indicator (RSSI) of a received message, this measurement may be used as an indication of distance from the sender. The received signal strength indicator (RSSI) is a measurement of the power present in a received radio signal.
- The nodes in a cluster may perform either of three roles: primary cluster head, secondary cluster head or sensing. Each cluster head performs activities such as scheduling of intra-cluster and inter-cluster communications, data aggregation, and data forwarding to the base station through multi-hop routing. The role of the secondary cluster head is to emulate the role of the primary cluster head in case of its failure. On the other hand, a sensing node maybe actively sensing the target area.
- The information sensed by the sensing nodes in a cluster are transmitted directly to their cluster head. The cluster head gathers data from the other nodes within its cluster, performs data aggregation/fusion and routes the data to the base station through other cluster head nodes. The base station in turn performs the key tasks of cluster formation, cluster head selection, and cluster head to cluster head QoS routing path construction.
- The base station has knowledge *via* internal global positioning system (GPS) of the position of all nodes inside the sensor field. The base station has a constant power supply and thus, has no energy constraints. Hence, it can also be used to perform functions that are energy intensive and can store past data. The base station can transmit directly to the nodes, however the nodes due to their limited power supply may not be able to communicate with the base station directly, except the nodes close to the base station.
- Radio Model: The energy required at the transmitter amplifier to guarantee an acceptable signal level at the receiver; when receiver and transmitter are separated by a distance d, $E_a(d)$ is:

$$E_a(d) = \begin{cases} \varepsilon_{FS}d^2, & d \leq d_o \\ \varepsilon_{TR}d^4, & d \geq d_o \end{cases} \tag{3.1}$$

here $\varepsilon_{FS}d^2$ and $\varepsilon_{TR}d^4$ denote the transmit amplification parameters corresponding to the free-space and two-ray models, respectively, and d_o is the threshold distance which is denoted by

$$d_o = \sqrt{\frac{\varepsilon_{FS}}{\varepsilon_{TR}}} \tag{3.2}$$

The topology of a Wireless Sensor Network may be described by a graph $G = (N, L)$, where N is the set of nodes and L is the set of links. The objectives are to

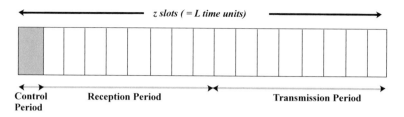

Fig. 3.2   TDMA frame structure for FTQAC

- Improve the lifetime of the network.
- Reduce the average end-to-end packet delay.
- Minimize the packet delivery ratio (PDR).
- Making the QoS Path Fault Tolerant.

The proposed protocol FTQAC incorporates QoS requirements like fault tolerance, delay, and bandwidth information during route establishment. The energy intensive tasks are delegated to the base station to improve the lifetime of the network. The operation of the protocol is split into phases. The first stage of FTQAC consists of the cluster splitting and primary cluster selection, the second phase involves the selection of the secondary cluster head. The last phase involves the formation of the QoS route from cluster head to the base station. TDMA (Time Division Multi Access) and spreading code are engaged to minimize inter-cluster interference to allow simultaneous transmissions in neighboring clusters. The TDMA structure for QBCDCP is shown in Fig. 3.2, where the frame length is of length L time units, segmented into z time slots, one of which is reserved for control and the remaining slots are partitioned for reception and transmission of data messages. The control period is used for transmission and reception of control messages related to clustering and routing information, state updates data requests and acknowledgments and neighbor discovery. To allow simultaneous transmissions in neighboring clusters and reduce inter-cluster interference, each cluster is assigned a different spreading code assumed to be orthogonal.

3.4   Cluster Setup and Primary Cluster Head Selection

In the proposed protocol, the cluster splitting and primary cluster head selection is accomplished by the Base Station [11] as shown in Algorithm 3.1.

Algorithm 3.1: Fault Tolerant Adaptive Clustering Algorithm (FTQAC)

---

1 Phase I : Cluster Setup and Primary Cluster Head Selection

Input: N Nodes, E_c Current energy level at each node
Output: Balanced clusters and Primary Cluster Heads

2 Calculate the average residual energy level of all the nodes ;
3 repeat

    (i) From set of nodes in N, choose two nodes ch_1 and ch_2 that have maximum separation distance between them ;

    (ii) Assign the remaining nodes to the closest cluster head ch_1 or ch_2, whichever being closer to from two clusters ;

    (iii) Balance the two clusters so that they have approximately the same number of nodes ;

    (iv) Split S into smaller sets s_1 and s_2 whose elements are the group members in step 3

4 until *N clusters with primary cluster heads have been selected*;
5 return N clusters, Primary cluster heads;

6 Phase II : Secondary Cluster Head Selection

Input: N clusters, Primary cluster heads
Output: Secondary Cluster Heads
7 Secondary Cluster Head Selection: 3.5
8 return Secondary Cluster Heads;

9 Phase III : QoS Route Establishment

Input: C (Set of primary cluster heads (PCHID)),
DPCHID (Destination Primary Cluster Head ID), BW_{req} (Minimum bandwidth required), D_{req} (End-to-end delay required), BW_{xy} (Bandwidth offered by link xy), D_{xy} (Delay associated with link xy), $E_a(d_{xy})$ (Power Amplifier energy of current cluster head, which is a function of the distance between the cluster heads and radio propagation model)
Output: Optimal QoS Path from Base Station to requesting Primary Cluster Head

10 for *each PCHID $\in$ C* **do**
11   **if** $BW_{xy} \geq BW_{req}$ **then**
12 $D_{Sum} = D_{Sum} + D_{xy}$;
13 $E_{aSum} = E_{aSum} + E_a(d_{xy})$;
14   Add PCHID to R;
15   **if** $PCHID == DPCHID$ **then**
16   **if** $D_{Sum} \leq D_{req}$ **then**
17   Add the path R and E_{aSum} of path to Q_R;
18   **else**
19   Discard R;

20   **else**
21   continue;

22   **else**
23   Discard R;

24 for *each R $\in Q_R$* **do**
25   Return Q_S with $Min\{E_{aSum}\}$

26 return Q_S;

3.5 Secondary Cluster Head Selection

In the next phase the primary cluster head has the role of identifying the secondary cluster head, the steps involved are shown below and illustrated in Fig. 3.3.

Fig. 3.3 Selection of secondary cluster head

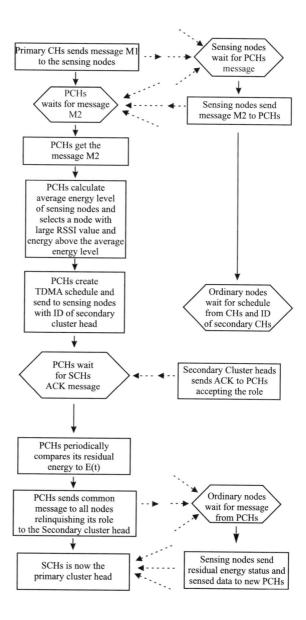

(i) Each new primary cluster head sends message M_1 to the sensing nodes in the cluster, the message contains the node's ID and a header to distinguish the message.

(ii) The sensing nodes record the Received Signal Strength Indicator (RSSI) of message M_1. The sensing nodes send message M_2 to the primary cluster. The message contains the node's ID, ID code of the primary cluster head, RSSI value of message received from the primary cluster head, and the current residual energy of the node.

(iii) The primary cluster head receives M_2 from ordinary nodes, the cluster head calculates the average residual energy level of all sensing nodes in the cluster. It selects a secondary cluster from one of the nodes which have the largest RSSI of message M_1 among the qualified nodes whose residual energy is more than the average residual energy of all nodes in the cluster.

(iv) The primary cluster head sets up the TDMA schedule and transmits the schedule to the secondary cluster head and the sensing nodes in the cluster. The role of the secondary cluster head is to emulate the primary cluster head in case of its failure.

(v) The primary cluster head sends a message M_3 periodically to the secondary cluster head informing its role and its current residual energy status. The secondary cluster head sends an ACK back to the primary cluster head on receiving the message.

(vi) When the residual energy of the primary cluster head is equal to or less than the E_t (threshold energy level) the primary cluster head relinquishes its role to the secondary cluster head by sending a common message to all nodes in the cluster.

(vii) The new primary cluster updates the base station of its delay, bandwidth and residual energy of the sensing nodes, it continues the functions of the cluster head using the same TDMA schedule.

(viii) The base station triggers re-clustering process only when more than one-third of the secondary cluster heads have reached their E_t, it also assigns the new E_t level for the next round based on the average residual energy of selected primary cluster heads. This process prevents frequent re-clustering and avoids excessive depletion of the cluster heads battery; this mechanism results in better power efficiency.

3.6   QoS Route Establishment

The desired QoS metrics for route establishment, i.e., delay, bandwidth of cluster head nodes and residual energy of the sensing nodes are aggregated and reported to the base station periodically. Delay and bandwidth are measured at cluster head nodes. The delay associated with traversing a particular cluster head is the time duration between entering the input queue and leaving the output queue of the cluster head

Table 3.1 Simulation parameters

Simulation parameters	Value
Number of sensors	100
Simulation topology	100×100 m
Distance to base station	25 m
Cluster radius	30m
Threshold distance (d_0)	75 m
Data packet size	300 bytes
Control packet size	25 bytes
Initial energy	2.0 Joules
Energy spent for send/receive	50 nJ/bit
Energy spent for data aggregation	5 nJ/bit
Free space model parameter	10 pJ/bit/m^2
Two-ray model parameter	0.0013 pJ/bit/m^2

(D_{xy}). Bandwidth is computed at each cluster head as the number of free time slots within each cluster head (BW_{xy}).

When a connection is desired, the base station sets up a QoS-based route Q_S between the cluster head where the connection is initiated through other cluster heads and finally ending at the base station as shown in Fig. 3.1. The base station finds the route which minimizes the delays and power along the path, and has a minimum bandwidth greater than or equal to the requested bandwidth (BW_{req}) as shown in Algorithm 3.1. The algorithm may produce more than one optimal path; the path having cluster heads with minimum required transmission energy (E_{aSum}) is chosen. After a route is chosen, the base station communicates it to the concerned cluster head nodes, which schedule the connection by specifying the required number of time slots to maintain it.

During the communication phase, when the primary cluster head is depleted of energy it transfers its role to the secondary cluster head. The primary cluster head is currently involved in the QoS path informs both the downstream cluster head, upstream cluster head, and the base station of its duty transfer and then relinquishes its role. The traffic is redirected to the new primary cluster and the QoS level is maintained throughout the duration of the connection.

3.7 Simulation Setup

To evaluate the proposed protocol, we carried out a simulation study using ns-2 [24] a discrete event simulator; the FTQAC implementation is obtained by modifying the popular LEACH [2, 3] ns-2 source code. The proposed protocol FTQAC is compared with QBCDCP. The simulation configuration consists of 100 nodes where each node

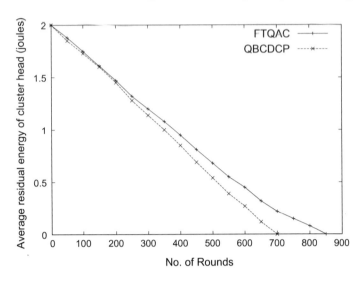

Fig. 3.4 Number of rounds versus average residual energy of cluster

is assigned an initial energy of 2 Joules, located in a 100 m^2 area. The base station is located 25 m from the sensor field. The end-to-end delay objective D_{req} is fixed at 10 s and BW_{req} was set at 16 Kbps by assigning each connection one out of 16 available TDMA time slots. Table 3.1 summarizes the simulation parameters. A comparison of the average residual energy of cluster heads, average end-to-end delay and packet delivery ratio (PDR) for different loads are obtained.

Figure 3.4 illustrates the role of the secondary cluster head in increasing the overall lifetime of the sensor network. In QBCDCP during the communication phase if the primary cluster head is depleted of energy, the entire cluster does not function and causes the WSN to become unstable and inconsistent. This problem can be overcome by the dual cluster head model. In FTQAC, the cluster continues to work reliably since the secondary cluster head takes the role of the primary cluster head when the threshold (E_t) energy is reached. In QBCDCP, the cluster formation is triggered frequently since the cluster head gets depleted of energy quickly.

In Fig. 3.4 the characteristics of both the protocols are similar initially since the energy level of the cluster heads are high, but during the later stage of simulation the average residual energy of primary cluster head in FTQAC is higher since the primary cluster head relinquishes its role to the secondary cluster head. This model of dual cluster head has the feature of fault-tolerance and improves the robustness of the WSN. From Fig. 3.4 it is observed that there is about 15% increase in the network lifetime using the dual cluster head model.

Figure 3.5 shows the average end-to-end delay for FTQAC and QBCDCP. In this evaluation, we change the packet arrival rate at the source node and measure the end-to-end delay. As expected, the increase in network load produces a higher queuing delay at each cluster head along a path, which gives a larger end-to-end delay. At a

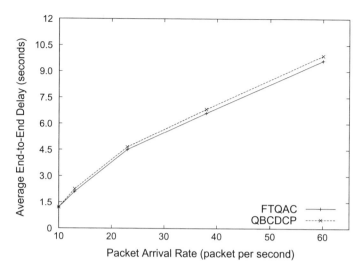

Fig. 3.5 Packet arrival rate versus average End-to-End delay

packet rate of 60 packets per second QBCDCP is unable to meet the delay objective of 10 seconds, due to the rapid depletion of energy in the cluster head; network congestion emerges at the cluster head because of limited energy and computing ability. The base station sets up paths based on the energy of the cluster heads. If a cluster head with low residual energy is selected for the QoS path, this results in drop of the link during the communication phase and affects the desired QoS. In FTQAC, the dual cluster head model ensures the necessary energy level and the bandwidth required for maintaining the link from base station to requesting cluster head node.

As depicted in Fig. 3.6, the packet delivery ratio (PDR), decreases as the packet arrival rate increases. The packet delivery ratio is defined as the number of packets generated by the source to the number of packets received by the destination node. It is observed that FTQAC performs marginally better than QBCDCP when the packet arrival rate is above 30 packets per second. In QBCDCP, as the packet arrival rate increases, the cluster head in the QoS path gets depleted of energy and the connection is terminated, triggering route repair and hence results in a lower PDR. In FTQAC, the role transfer from primary cluster head to secondary cluster head ensures that the scheduled connection is not dropped, thereby maintaining the packet delivery ratio.

3.8 Summary

This chapter presents a Fault Tolerant QoS Adaptive Clustering Algorithm (FTQAC) protocol. The protocol achieves QoS routing in Wireless Sensor Networks by using delay and transmission energy as the routing metrics. It also ensures that the band-

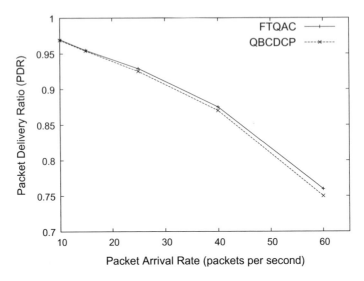

Fig. 3.6 Packet arrival rate versus packet delivery ratio

width objective of the application is met. The protocol achieves fault tolerance through a dual cluster head mechanism and guarantees the desired QoS. Evaluated results show an increase in lifetime of the WSN. The FTQAC provides an improvements of up to 15% increase in lifetime when compared to QBCDCP. The FTQAC is a feasible solution to the QoS fault tolerant routing problem in power constrained Wireless Sensor Networks.

References

1. O. Abraham, Fapojuwo and Alejandra Cano-Tinoco: energy consumption and message delay analysis of QoS enhanced base station controlled dynamic clustering protocol for wireless sensor networks. IEEE Trans. Wirel. Commun. **8**(10), 5366–5374 (2009)
2. W.R. Heinzelman, A. Chandrakasan, H. Balakrishnan, Energy efficient communication protocol for wireless microsensor networks, in *Proceedings of the 33rd Annual Hawaii International Conference on System Sciences*, vol. 2 (2000), pp. 2–11
3. W.B. Heinzelman, A.P. Chandrakasan, H. Balakrishnan, An application-specific protocol architecture for wireless microsensor networks. IEEE Trans. Wirel. Commun. **1**(4), 606–670 (2002)
4. A. Manjeshwar, D.P. Agrawal, TEEN: a protocol for enhanced efficiency in wireless sensor networks, in *Proceedings of the 15th International Workshop on Parallel and Distributed Computing Issues in Wireless Networks and Mobile Computing* (San Francisco, CA, 2001) pp. 2009–2015
5. A. Manjeshwar, D.P. Agrawal, A hybrid protocol for efficient routing and comprehensive information retrieval in wireless sensor networks, in *Proceedings of the 2nd International Workshop on Parallel and Distributed Computing Issues in Wireless Networks and Mobile Computing* (Ft. Lauderdale, Fl, 2002), pp. 195–202

6. S. Lindsey, C.S. Raghavendra, PEGASIS: power efficient gathering in sensor information systems, in *Proceedings of the IEEE Aerospace Conference, Big Sky, Montana*, vol. 3 (2002), pp. 1125–1130

7. Ossama Younis, Sonia Fahmy, HEED: a hybrid, energy-efficient, distributed clustering approach for ad hoc sensor networks. IEEE Trans. Mob. Comput. **3**(4), 366–379 (2004)

8. G. Smaragdakis, I. Matta, A. Bestavros, SEP: a stable election protocol for clustered heterogeneous wireless sensor networks, in *Proceedings of the 2nd International Workshop on Sensor and Actor Network Protocols and Applications* (2004), pp. 56–66

9. V. Loscri, S. Marano, G. Morabito, A two-levels hierarchy for low-energy adaptive clustering hierarchy (TL-LEACH), in *Proceedings of the VTC2005* (Dallas, USA, 2005), pp. 1809–1813

10. W. Chen, W. Li, H. Shou, B. Yuan, A QoS-based adaptive clustering algorithm for wireless sensor networks, in *Proceedings of the 2006 IEEE International Conference on Mechatronics and Automation* (Luoyang, China, 2006) pp. 1947–1952

11. S.D. Muruganathan, D.C.F. Ma, R.I. Bhasin, A.O. Fapojuwo, A centralized energy-efficient routing protocol for wireless sensor networks. IEEE Commun. Mag. **43**(3), S8–S13 (2005)

12. H. Haiping, W. Ruchuan, Clustered-control algorithm for wireless multimedia sensor network communications, in *Proceedings International Conference on Communications and Mobile Computing* (2010), pp. 264–268

13. P. Ji, C. Wu, Y. Zhang, F. Chen, A low-energy adaptive clustering routing protocol of wireless sensor networks, in *Proceedings of the International Conference on Wireless Communications, Networking and Mobile Computing (WiCOM)* (2011), pp. 1–4

14. J. Feng, X. Yu, Z. Liu, C. Wang, A QoS enhanced routing protocol in wireless sensor networks, in *Proceedings of the International Conference on Computer Communications and Networks (ICCCN)* (2011), pp. 1–6

15. G.H. EkbataniFard, R. Monsefi, M.R. Akbarzadeh-T, M.H. Yaghmaee, A multi-objective genetic algorithm based approach for energy efficient QoS-routing in two-tiered wireless sensor networks, in *Proceedings of the International Symposium on Wireless Pervasive Computing (ISWPC)* (2010), pp. 80–85

16. J. Ben-othman, L. Mokdad, B. Yahya, An energy efficient priority-based QoS MAC protocol for wireless sensor networks, in *Proceedings of the International Conference on Communications (ICC)* (2011), pp. 1–6

17. N. Aslam, W. Phillips, G.A Safdar, Worst case bounds of a cluster-based mac protocol for wireless sensor networks, in *Proceedings of the Wireless Telecommunications Symposium (WTS)* (2012), pp. 1–6

18. T. Melodia, I.F. Akyildiz, Cross-layer quality of service support for uwb wireless multimedia sensor networks, in *Proceedings of the 27th IEEE INFOCOM 2008* (2008), pp. 2038–2046

19. M. Noori, M. Ardakani, Lifetime analysis of random Event-Driven clustered wireless sensor networks. IEEE Trans. Mob. Comput. **10**(10), 1448–1458 (2011)

20. M. Yao, C. Lin, Y. Tian, L. Wu, Y. Chen, Energy and delay minimization in cluster-based wireless sensor networks, in *Proceedings of the IEEE International Conference on Green Computing and Communications (GreenCom)* (2012) pp. 588–594

21. P.T.A. Quang, D.-S. Kim, An energy efficient clustering in heterogeneous wireless sensor and actuators networks, in *Proceedings of the IEEE Globecom Workshops* (2012), pp. 524–528

22. I.-R. Chen, A.P. Speer, M. Eltoweissy, Adaptive fault-tolerant QoS control algorithms for maximizing system lifetime of query-based wireless sensor networks. IEEE Trans. Dependable Secur. Comput. **8**(2), 161–176 (2011)

23. T.S. Prakash, K.B. Raja, K.R. Venugopal, S.S. Iyengar, L.M. Patnaik, Fault tolerant QoS adaptive clustering for wireless sensor networks, in *Proceedings of the Ninth International Conference on Wireless Communication and Sensor Networks WCSN'13, Springer LNEE-7818*, vol. 299 (2013), pp. 167–175

24. NS-2, http://www.isi.edu/nsnam/ns/

Chapter 4
ETXTD: ETX and RTT Delay Based Fault Detection Algorithm for WSNs

Abstract In order to sustain QoS when sensor nodes deteriorate and malfunction, node fault detection and recovery techniques are necessary. An Expected Transmission Count and Round Trip Time Delay (ETXTD) based Fault Detection Algorithm is proposed in this chapter that is able to identify working and faulty sensors in a computationally effective manner.

4.1 Introduction

Wireless Sensor Networks by nature are error-prone and have low reliability, sensor nodes encounter various faults and failures during their operation. Failures range from simple crash faults (where a node becomes temporarily inactive) to battery exhaustion resulting in node failures. The nature of real-time applications creates significant challenges for sensor networks to maintain a high Quality of Service. Therefore, efficient fault detection and detachment have become essential for WSNs and we address these challenges in this chapter.

Duche et al. [1] propose a mechanism to maintain better QoS under node failure, by identifying and detaching faults. In this method, faulty sensor nodes are detected by measuring the Round Trip Delay time of discrete Round Trip Paths (RTDP) and comparing them with threshold values.

The QoS of the network is affected by the failure of sensor nodes. Probability of sensor node failure increases with an increasing number of sensors. In order to maintain QoS paths under failure conditions, identifying and detaching such faults becomes essential.

Expected Transmission Count and Round Trip Time Delay (ETXTD) based Fault Detection Algorithm is able to identify working and faulty sensors in a computationally effective manner. The traffic is redirected to the working sensors and the QoS level is maintained throughout the duration of the connection as shown in Fig. 4.1.

© Springer Nature Singapore Pte Ltd. 2020
K. R. Venugopal et al., *QoS Routing Algorithms for Wireless Sensor Networks*,
https://doi.org/10.1007/978-981-15-2720-3_4

Fig. 4.1 Qos routing path
when some sensor nodes fail

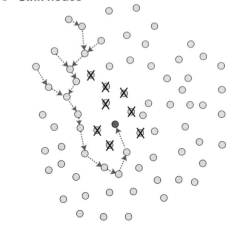

○ Sensor nodes

● Sink nodes

☒ Dead/Faulty Node

4.2   Related Works

Chen et al. [2] propose an adaptive fault tolerant quality of service (QoS) control algorithm that is based on a hop-by-hop data transmission method that employs path and source redundancy, which aid in application QoS demands and improve the lifetime of the system.

Path redundancy technique to detect faulty sensor node is suggested in [3, 4]. Redundancy multiplies the energy consumption and lowers the number of right responses in sensor network lifetime. Many redundant paths in the sensor networks affect the rate of fault detection. In [5], link failure detection based on monitoring cycles (MCs) and monitoring paths (MPs) is presented. The constraints of this method are monitoring locations and separate wavelength for each monitoring cycle.

Lee et al. [6] present a distributed fault detection algorithm for Wireless Sensor Networks. Faulty sensor nodes are found based on the correlation between neighboring nodes and publishing of the result contrived at each node. Time redundancy is employed to endure short term faults in sensing and communication process. To speed up the process, a sliding window is selected with storage for historical values. Cluster head failure recovery algorithm used in [7] to identify the faulty node has data loss issues, which develop on transfer of cluster head.

Lau et al. [8] developed a centralized hardware fault detection process for a structured Wireless Sensor Network (WSN) based on a Centralized Naive Bayes Detector (CNBD), which investigates the end-to-end transmission time at the sink. In this method, computation is not executed in individual sensor node and has no added power load to the sensor node.

Yang et al. [9] present an uncertainty-based distributed fault detection through aided judgment of neighbors for Wireless Sensor Networks. The algorithm examines the genuine sensing measurement loss and adopts Markov processes for padding in lost data. The knowledge of evidence fusion rules established on information entropy theory and degree of disagreement function aids to raise the efficiency of fault detection.

Mitra et al. [10] present an energy aware fault tolerant framework in Wireless Sensor Network. Fault detection algorithm, improved network lifetime, and self fault checking in Wireless Sensor Networks are proposed.

Mahapatro et al. [11] introduce a multi-objective based particle swarm optimization (2LB-MOPSO) algorithm for solving the multi-objective problem of intermittent fault detection. A fuzzy logic based approach is employed to select the leading compromised result on the Pareto front. In [12], they present an online fault diagnosis algorithm for Wireless Sensor Networks, that considers the probability of faults in different parts of the sensor networks.

Lee et al. [13] propose an Adaptive routing protocol for fast Recovery (ARF) from large-scale Failure, to restore a network instantly after failures over broad areas. ARF identifies faults by estimating the packet failure from parent nodes, and the algorithm reduces the routing gap to alert the neighbor nodes of the fault.

Prakash et al. [14] propose and analyze an Energy-Efficient Fault Tolerant QoS Adaptive Clustering Algorithm (FTQAC) for Wireless sensor networks suitable to support real-time traffic. The protocol achieves fault tolerance and energy efficiency through a dual cluster head mechanism and guarantees the desired QoS by including delay and bandwidth parameters in the route selection process.

Shin et al. [15] present a fault node recovery algorithm for WSN on the concept of grade diffusion with a genetic algorithm. The algorithm aids in substituting lesser sensor nodes and utilize the routing paths, improving the WSN lifetime, and decreasing the substitution cost.

Chatzigiannakis et al. [16] propose an anomaly detection approach that combines data collected from various nodes in a distributed sensor network. Stress is given on data correctness induced by malicious nodes. The proposed approach employs Principal Component Analysis together on various metrics collected from different sensors. This method combines related sensor data in a shared manner to detect faults among many sensors and assimilate the outcome from multiple groups of nodes.

Duche et al. [1] propose a mechanism to maintain better QoS under node failure, by identifying and detaching faults. In this method, faulty sensor nodes are exposed by measuring the Round Trip Delay time of discrete Round Trip Paths (RTDP) and comparing them with the original values. The proposed ETXTD Algorithm in this paper addresses the shortcomings in [1] with respect to time complexity and considers ETX (Expected Transmission Count) [17] metric to improve fault detection speed.

4.3 System Model and Problem Definition

The topology of a Wireless Sensor Network is described by a graph $G = (N, L)$, where N is the set of nodes and L is the set of links. The objectives are to

- Identify and isolate malfunctioning and dead sensor nodes.
- Sustain the QoS path between source and destination.

In our network model, we assume the following:

- The wireless sensor nodes consist of N sensor nodes and a sink, the sensors are distributed in a random manner in the field and are assumed to be stationary.
- The N sensor nodes are powered by a nonrenewable on board energy source.
- The network density is assumed to be high enough to prevent the void situation.

4.4 Algorithm

The Algorithm consists of the following modules: (a) Estimation of Expected Transmission Count Metric (ETX) Metric; (b) Estimation of Round Trip Time (RTT) and Round Trip Path (RTP); and (c) Detection of Faulty Sensor Node.

4.4.1 Estimation of Expected Transmission Count (ETX) Metric

The ETX (Expected Transmission Count Metric) [17] of a link is the predicted number of data transmissions required to send a packet over that link, including retransmissions. The goal of using ETX is to find the route with the highest probability of packet delivery, instead of the shortest path. It is one of the favored routing metrics because it has good accuracy in determining link quality. The ETX between two immediate nodes i and j is defined as

$$ETX(i, j) = \frac{1}{d_f \times d_r} \tag{4.1}$$

where d_f and d_r are the forward and the reverse delivery ratios of the link from node i to j. The forward delivery ratio, d_f is the measured probability that a data packet successfully arrives at the recipient; the reverse delivery ratio, d_r is the probability that the ACK packet is successfully received. The delivery ratios d_f and d_r are estimated using dedicated link probe packets. Each node broadcasts link probes of a fixed size, at an average period.

Calculation of a links ETX requires both d_f and d_r. Each probe sent by a node i contains the number of probe packets received by i from each of its neighbors during the last w seconds. This allows each neighbor to calculate the d_f to i whenever it receives a probe from i. The ETX computation considers both forward and reverse directions because of data and ACK-frame transmissions.

4.4.2 Estimation of Round Trip Time (RTT) and Round Trip Path (RTP)

This metric is based on measuring the round trip delay seen by unicast probes between neighboring nodes. To calculate RTT, a node sends a probe packet carrying a time stamp to each of its neighbors. Each neighbor immediately responds to the probe with a probe acknowledgment, echoing the time stamp. This enables the sending node to measure round trip time to each of its neighbors.

RTT is based upon the numbers of sensor nodes present in the Round Trip Path (RTP) (i.e., several nodes in a path, ideally three) and the euclidean distance between them. The fault detection analysis time increases immensely with larger numbers of sensor nodes. Choosing minimum numbers of sensor nodes in the RTP lowers the Round Trip Time. The RTP in WSNs is formed by grouping minimum three sensor nodes x_1, x_2, and x_3.

$$\eta_{RTD} = \eta_{x1} + \eta_{x2} + \eta_{x3} \tag{4.2}$$

The numbers of RTPs are decreased by selecting only discrete paths in WSNs. Discrete RTPs are selected from sequential linear RTPs. They are selected by ignoring the two consecutive paths, after each selected linear path. In this way, RTPs are selected in discrete steps of three as each RTP consists of three sensor nodes [1]. The equation to select the discrete RTPs is

$$T_{RTP} = Q + C \tag{4.3}$$

where $Q = |N/3|$ is the quotient and N is numbers of sensor nodes in the Wireless Sensor Networks and C is 0 if the remainder is 0, otherwise, it is 1. This helps in reducing the number of RTPs selected for the sensor network.

4.4.3 Detection of Faulty Sensor Node

ETX and RTT are used together to detect working and faulty sensor nodes. Discrete RTPs with ETX of the links between three sensor nodes explained above are used to determine the faults in the WSNs. In the first stage, the threshold values of ETX and RTT time are determined and in the next stage, the faults are detected. Initially, all the nodes in the network are treated as working. The ETX of the links connecting the three nodes is obtained, then the discrete RTPs are selected by incrementing the source node value by three and their respective RTD times are collected. These values serve as a base for detecting the faulty node.

In [1], instantaneous RTT delay of discrete RTPs is compared with the threshold time. Discrete RTPs whose RTT delay is found to be larger than threshold time is then evaluated in detail. This individual discrete RTP is inspected in three stages to detect the exact position of the fault. If x_1 is the source node of the discrete RTP with nodes x_2 and x_3 as the next nodes, i.e., $RTP_{x1} : x_1 \rightarrow x_2 \rightarrow x_3$.

The faulty node could be present in either of the three nodes; further RTPs constituting these sensor nodes need to be inspected to identify the faulty node. RTPs constituting second and third node in the RTPs are $RTP_{x2} : x_2 \rightarrow x_3 \rightarrow x_4$ and $RTP_{x3} : x_3 \rightarrow x_4 \rightarrow x_5$. The RTT delay of these RTPs are recorded sequentially. Using the RTD time, these RTPs are analyzed to detect the faulty sensor by comparing the RTD times of respective RTPs with threshold time. This approach requires three steps to locate the exact position of the fault.

Algorithm 4.1: ETXTD: Expected Transmission Count and Round Trip Time Delay

---

Input: $RTPs$, RTT of $RTPs$, ETX of links
Output: Faulty or dead node

1 **while** *not last RTP* **do**
2 | **if** $(\eta_{RTD_{x_1}} > \eta_T)$ *and* $(\eta_{RTD_{x_2}} == \eta_T)$ **then**
3 | | **if** $(ETX_{x_1} > ETX_t)$ *and* $(ETX_{x_2} == ETX_t)$ **then**
4 | | |__ Node x_1 is Faulty;
5 | | **if** $(\eta_{RTD_{x_1}} == \infty)$ *and* $(ETX_{x_1} == \infty)$ **then**
6 | | |__ Node x_1 is Dead;
7 | **if** $(\eta_{RTD_{x_1}} > \eta_T)$ *and* $(\eta_{RTD_{x_2}} > \eta_T)$ **then**
8 | | **if** $(ETX_{x_1} == ETX_t)$ *and* $(ETX_{x_3} > ETX_t)$ **then**
9 | | |__ Node x_3 is Faulty;
10 | | **if** $(ETX_{x_3} == \infty)$ **then**
11 | | |__ Node x_3 is Dead;
12 | **if** $(ETX_{x_1} > ETX_t)$ *and* $(ETX_{x_2} > ETX_t)$ *and* $(ETX_{x_3} == ETX_t)$ **then**
13 | |__ Node x_2 is Faulty;
14 | **if** $(ETX_{x_2} == \infty)$ **then** Node x_2 is Dead;

In our approach, we consider the ETX of the links between $x_1 \rightarrow x_2 \rightarrow x_3$ and the RTT delay of RTPs of the first and second nodes only, i.e., RTP_{x_1} and RTP_{x_2}. It is shown in [18], that ETX is a better metric in terms of throughput than RTT delay. RTT delay metric performs poorly mainly because of load-sensitivity which leads to route oscillations.

Combining the ETX of the links and RTT delay of discrete RTPs, the faulty node can be detected quickly and efficiently using only two RTPs, i.e.,

(a) If RTT delay, i.e., $\eta_{RTD_{x_1}}$ of RTP_{x_1} is greater than RTT delay threshold η_T and RTT delay of RTP_{x_2}, i.e., $\eta_{RTD_{x_2}}$ is equal to η_T, then ETX_{x_1} is greater than ETX threshold ETX_t and ETX_{x_2} is equal to threshold ETX_t, then node x_1 is faulty. However if $\eta_{RTD_{x_1}}$ and ETX_{x_1} is equal to ∞, then node x_1 if dead.

(b) If $\eta_{RTD_{x_1}}$ and $\eta_{RTD_{x_2}}$ are both greater than η_T, then ETX_{x_1} is equal to ETX_t and ETX_{x_3} is greater than ETX_t, then node x_3 is faulty or if ETX_{x_3} equal to ∞ then node x_3 is dead. However if ETX_{x_1} and ETX_{x_2} is greater than threshold ETX_t and ETX_{x_3} is equal to ETX_t then node x_2 is faulty. If ETX_{x_2} equal to ∞ then node x_2 is dead.

The process is repeated until the last RTP is analyzed in the WSN. The ETXTD method is detailed in Algorithm 4.1. This approach is better than the RTDP method which requires three RTPs to determine the faulty node. By considering the ETX and RTT delay of RTPs of the first and second nodes leads to optimization and aids in reducing the fault detection time when the WSNs are large.

4.4.4 Performance Evaluation

To evaluate the proposed protocol, we carried out a simulation study using ns-2 [19]. The proposed protocol ETXTD is compared with RTDP. The simulation configuration consists of 100 nodes located in a 100 m^2 area. The source generated a CBR flow of 1 packet/second with a packet size of 150 bytes using QoS protocol SPEED [20]. Table 4.1 summarizes the simulation parameters.

In first simulation study, we vary the number of nodes in the WSN and determine the time taken to detect the fault for both the protocols. The performance using the ETX+RTD metric is found to be better than just using the RTD metric. From Fig. 4.2, it is observed that the time to identify a faulty node increases with the number of nodes in the network. The performance of the Round Trip Delay based Fault Detection technique is slow; the protocol employs three phases using round trip paths to detect the fault. However, when ETX is used in conjunction with the Round Trip Time delays, the faulty node can be detected in reduced time complexity.

In the next study, to evaluate the robustness of ETXTD, in a failing network, the total number of nodes in the sensor network is fixed to 100. For each end-to-end

Table 4.1 Simulation parameters

Simulation parameters	Value
Number of nodes	100
Simulation topology	100×100 m
Traffic	CBR
Routing protocol	SPEED
Payload size	150 Bytes
Transmission range	1 m
Initial battery energy	1.0 Joule

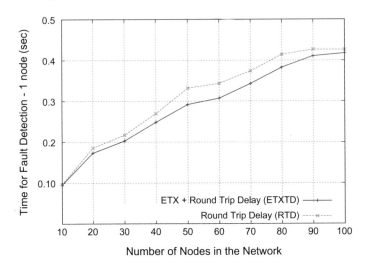

Fig. 4.2 Comparisons of fault detection time—for 1 Node versus Number of nodes in network

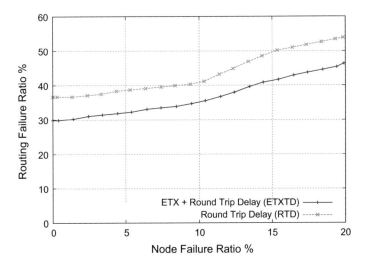

Fig. 4.3 Routing failure ratio versus Node failure ratio

packet delivery path, a certain percentage of nodes are randomly selected to turn off. The percentage of failed nodes is varied from 5 to 20% to investigate the effect of node failure on the routing path.

A routing failure ratio, which is defined as the percentage that a packet cannot be delivered by the protocols from the source to the destination, is used to measure the effectiveness of the fault detection techniques used in the QoS routing protocol. Figure 4.3 shows that routing failure ratios of both ETXTD and RTDP ascend as the node failure ratio increases. When the routing protocol uses RTDP, it is unable to find the failures quickly and the routing paths discovered by them are broken due to node failure and hence reduces the number of packets reaching the destination. However, ETXTD is robust in finding the failed nodes and sustains the QoS paths, hence it is able to reduce the routing failure ratio.

4.5 Summary

An Expected Transmission Count and Round Trip Time Delay (ETXTD) based Fault Detection Algorithm is proposed in this chapter that is able to identify working and faulty sensors in a computationally effective manner. Two RTPs are sufficient to detect the faulty sensor node. Scalability of the method has been verified by implementing it on WSNs. The method is an effective method to speedily detect and separate the malfunctioning nodes from the network and sustain the QoS paths.

References

1. R.N. Duche, N.P. Sarwade, Sensor node failure detection based on round trip delay and paths in WSNs. Sens. J., IEEE **14**(2), 455–464 (2014)
2. I.-R. Chen, A.P. Speer, M. Eltoweissy, Adaptive fault-tolerant QoS control algorithms for maximizing system lifetime of query-based wireless sensor networks. IEEE Trans. Dependable Secur. Comput. **8**(2), 161–176 (2011)
3. C.-C. Song, C.-F. Feng, C.-H. Wang, D.-C. Liaw, Simulation and experimental analysis of a ZigBee sensor network with fault detection and reconfiguration mechanism, in *Control Conference (ASCC), 2011 8th Asian*, (2011), pp. 659–664
4. A. Mojoodi, M. Mehrani, F. Forootan, R. Farshidi, Redundancy effect on fault tolerance in wireless sensor networks. Glob. J. Comput. Sci. Technol. **11**(6), 35–40 (2011)
5. S.S. Ahuja, S. Ramasubramanian, M.M. Krunz, Single-link failure detection in all-optical networks using monitoring cycles and paths. Netw., IEEE/ACM Trans. **17**(4), 1080–1093 (2009)
6. M.-H. Lee, Y.-H. Choi, Fault detection of wireless sensor networks. Comput. Commun. **31**(14), 3469–3475 (2008)
7. A. Akbari, A. Dana, A. Khademzadeh, N. Beikmahdavi, Fault detection and recovery in wireless sensor network using clustering. IJWMN **3**(1), 130–138 (2011)
8. B.C. Lau, E.W. Ma, T.W. Chow, probabilistic fault detector for wireless sensor network. Expert Syst. Appl. **41**(8), 3703–3711 (2014)
9. Y. Yang, Z. Gao, H. Zhou, X. Qiu, An uncertainty-based distributed fault detection mechanism for wireless sensor networks. Sensors **14**(5), 7655–7683 (2014)
10. S. Mitra, A. De Sarkar, Energy aware fault tolerant framework in wireless sensor network. Appl. Innov. Mob. Comput. (AIMoC) **2014**, 139–145 (2014)
11. A. Mahapatro, P.M. Khilar, Detection and diagnosis of node failure in wireless sensor networks: a multi-objective optimization approach. Swarm Evol. Comput. **13**, 74–84 (2013)
12. A. Mahapatro, P.M. Khilar, Online distributed fault diagnosis in wireless sensor networks. Wirel. Pers. Commun. **71**(3), 1931–1960 (2013)
13. J.-H. Lee, I.-B. Jung, Speedy routing recovery protocol for large failure tolerance in wireless sensor networks. Sensors **10**(4), 3389–3410 (2010)

14. T.S. Prakash, K.B. Raja, K.R. Venugopal, S.S. Iyengar, L.M. Patnaik, Fault tolerant QoS adaptive clustering for wireless sensor networks, in *Proceedings Ninth International Conference on Wireless Communication and Sensor Networks WCSN'13, Springer LNEE-7818* vol. 299 (2013), pp. 167–175
15. H.-C. Shih, J.-H. Ho, B.-Y. Liao, J.-S. Pan, Fault node recovery algorithm for a wireless sensor network. Sens. J., IEEE **13**(7), 2683–2689 (2013)
16. V. Chatzigiannakis, S. Papavassiliou, Diagnosing anomalies and identifying faulty nodes in sensor networks. Sens. J., IEEE **7**(5), 637–645 (2007)
17. D.S. Couto, D. Aguayo, J. Bicket, R. Morris, A high-throughput path metric for multi-hop wireless routing, in *Proceedings MobiCom* (2003), pp. 134–146
18. R. Draves, J. Padhye, B. Zill, Comparison of routing metrics for static multi-hop wireless networks. SIGCOMM Comput. Commun. Rev. **34**(4), 133–144 (2004)
19. NS-2, http://www.isi.edu/nsnam/ns/
20. T. He, J.A. Stankovic, L. Chenyang, T.F. Abdelzaher, A spatiotemporal protocol for wireless sensor network. IEEE Trans. Parallel Distrib. Syst. **16**(10), 995–1006 (2005)

Chapter 5
DQTSM: Distributed Qos in Time Synchronized MAC Protocol for WSNs

Abstract In this chapter, we have designed a Distributed Qos in Time Synchronized MAC (DQTSM) protocol to reduce the time synchronization of the entire network with minimum synchronization messages overhead for WSNs. The combined effect of low synchronization error and low synchronization messages decrease the amount of consumption of energy resulting in an increase in the lifetime of WSNs. The simulation results confirm that DQTSM protocol has low synchronization error, synchronization message overheads, and lower energy consumption as compared to FTSP and TTS.

5.1 Introduction

Time synchronization is an important parameter for an event action, coordination among nodes and time measurements for common time on distributed sensor nodes. We have designed a Distributed QoS in Time Synchronized MAC (DQTSM) protocol that is a primary service for coordination of scattered sensor nodes regularly by exchanging messages in the WSNs applications in home automation, industrial automation, military, and medical, etc. The DQTSM is important for the operation of WSNs in considering local clocks at each sensor node that needs to be synchronized with reference to the clock at the Master node. The synchronization error is due to the non-deterministic random time delay for a message transfer between the Master node and the Receiver nodes. DQTSM reduces sources of synchronization error at the Medium Access Control layer in channel contention and reduces the network traffic required for time synchronization.

5.2 Related Works

Time synchronization is a fundamental concept for improving device performance. To identify the correct event time, sensor nodes are synchronized with the clock. Time synchronization is a serious problem of infrastructure in any densely distributed

© Springer Nature Singapore Pte Ltd. 2020
K. R. Venugopal et al., *QoS Routing Algorithms for Wireless Sensor Networks*,
https://doi.org/10.1007/978-981-15-2720-3_5

network and has been discussed in terms of different parameters such as synchronization error, accuracy, fault tolerance, scalability, and energy efficiency. Mock et al. [1] extend IEEE 802.11 Master Slave protocol to Reference Broadcast Synchronization (RBS) where continuous clock connection is carried out. The correction is done every clock tick and hence expensive.

Elson et al. [2] provide a relative time-frame for conversion between the local clocks of different nodes and can be used to synchronize nodes to an external timesource such as GPS. Contention may cause unpredictable delays before a message is broadcasted; once a message is transmitted, it is received by all nodes in the sender's neighborhood almost instantaneously. The advantage of Reference Broadcast Synchronization (RBS) is that it allows a set of receivers in a broadcast network to accurately estimate each other's clock values.

Ganeriwal et al. [3] develope the Time Synchronization protocol for Sensor Network (TPSN) that uses timestamps at the MAC layer resulting in reduced retransmissions. Greunen et al. [4] propose a Lightweight Time Synchronization (LTS) where low time accuracy is tolerated and is similar to TPSN.

Dai et al. [5] introduce two time synchronization protocols namely; A beacon synchronization message is sent to a designated node that broadcasts over the entire network. Individual-based Time Request (ITR) and Hierarchy Referencing Time Synchronization (HRTS), which are similar to RBS.

Gao et al. [6] develop a method for enhancing time synchronization suitable for use in adhoc sensor networks where processing power is constrained. The technique is local and uses Bayesian estimation. Visweswara et al. [7] propose strategies for adaptation of the sleeping schedule, almost all of these approaches assume that the packet arrival follows a constant-rate Poisson distributed arrival model or the periodic arrival model. Observing the weakness of the two kinds of arrival models, the quasi-periodic arrival model has been recently introduced in studying the sleep scheduling.

Maroti et al. [8] achieve time synchronization with very low error rate. It is also scalable up to hundreds of nodes due to its flooding property. This Flooding Time Synchronization Protocol (FTSP) is robust to network links and nodes failure. FTSP uses MAC layer time-stamping with several jitter reducing techniques and estimation of the clock drift to obtain high precision. Ye et al. [9] suggest synchronous channel polling to reduce energy wastage and also a multi-hop streaming scheme to handle bursty traffic towards base stations. During the contention window, only the contending senders are awake and only the winner of the contention is awake for more than a short poll.

Ganeriwal et al. [10] propose the Rate Adaptive Time Synchronization (RATS) algorithm; the synchronization interval is adjusted based on the computed prediction uncertainty. When the indicated uncertainty is higher than a threshold ηmax, the synch interval is halved to increase the synchronization frequency and when the indicated uncertainty is lower than a threshold $\eta min \leq \eta max$, the synch interval is doubled to decrease the synchronization frequency.

Su et al. [11] focus on nodes employing Time-Diffusion Synchronization protocol (TDP); it periodically self-determines to become master nodes periodically self-determine to become master. Master nodes then engage neighboring nodes in a peer evaluation procedure to isolate problem nodes. Timing information messages are broadcasted from master nodes and then rebroadcasted by the diffused master nodes for a fixed number of hops, forming a radial tree structure. This approach is fully distributed, but it does not compensate for the clock drift. Li et al. [12] present node-based and cluster-based synchronization which is not appropriate for large Wireless Sensor Networks. In the diffusion method, a node sets its clock by averaging the clock time of its neighbors.

Younis et al. [13] design a Hybrid Energy-Efficient Distributed clustering approach (HEED) for adhoc networks, the cluster head selection is primarily based on the energy of each sensor node. The clustering operations involve a number of rounds of repetitions, each repetition exploiting some probabilistic methods for nodes to elect to become a cluster head. HEED, a distributed protocol, ensures that each node can either elect to become a cluster head or it can join a cluster within its range.

Noh et al. [14] propose the Maximum Likelihood Estimator (MLE) of clock offset in a two-way message swap model, where the clock offsets of two nodes remain equal during the synchronization period. Jia et al. [15] propose a routing protocol called the Clustering-Base Expanding Ring Routing Protocol (CBERRP) which mainly focuses on the network layer while integrating factors from other layers to increase the performance efficiency. Li et al. [16] propose Average Time Synchronization Protocol (ATSP) which provide network-wide average time synchronization for WSNs; random time is the delay and clock skew are considered, while satisfying synchronization error tolerance.

Kim et al. [17] develop a Energy-Efficient Time Synchronization (EETS) scheme that consists of level discovery phase and synchronization phase. The broadcast technique used here reduces the number of messages required for synchronization. Albu et al. [18] propose an IEEE 1588 PBS Hybrid Protocol which minimizes energy consumption and ensures accurate synchronization in Wireless Sensor Networks. Wu et al. [19] focus on a common time frame to different nodes, which supports time-based channel sharing and coordinated sleep/wake-up node scheduling techniques. Clock synchronization is a critical function in WSNs and their performance is assessed using common statistical signal processing methods.

Wu et al. [20] present a wake/sleep scheduling algorithm for low-duty cycle WSNs which focuses on estimating the threshold of messages from each individual sensor node to minimize the expected consumption of energy and to meet QoS requirement of the applications. Wang et al. [21] present a Two-hop Time Synchronization (TTS) protocol for WSNs which decreases the synchronization overhead and supports the entire network because it divides the synchronization hops. The idea of designing TTS for small synchronization hops is to reduce overhead. This algorithm extends the single-hop to multi-hop synchronization.

5.3 System Model and Problem Definition

Consider a N number of autonomous nodes out of which one node is assigned the sender node (SN) and all other nodes are receiver nodes (RN_i), $i \in \{1, 2, \ldots, (N-1)\}$. All the receiving nodes need to send the response at different times in order to avoid collisions after receiving the time synchronization message from the sender node. The communication range of a sensor node is assumed to be less than a few hundred meters and a communication channel exists between each node with other sensor nodes. The procedure of time synchronization for distributed systems is to provide a standard notion of time across the WSNs. Time synchronization refers to the issue of synchronization of clocks across a number of sensor nodes that are connected to one another over one-hop WSNs as shown in Fig. 5.1. The main objectives of the proposed work are to

(i) Minimize the Synchronization error.
(ii) Provide Correct links between two or more sensor nodes.
(iii) Reduce Synchronization messages and
(iv) Reduce Energy consumption.

The assumptions are

(i) The sensor nodes are randomly deployed.
(ii) Clock initial values and clock rate are randomly assigned.
(iii) Each sensor node has a fixed transmission range.

In this section, we develop a Distributed QoS in Time Synchronized MAC (DQTSM) protocol that synchronizes the Wireless Sensor Network nodes with reference to the Master Node. A random time delay for message transmission between Master node and Receiver nodes can cause a synchronization error. The system model consists of N number of sensor nodes, which communicate using radio transmission. The sensor nodes in the network have an unique ID and they can identify each other.

Fig. 5.1 One-hop time synchronization sensor network topology

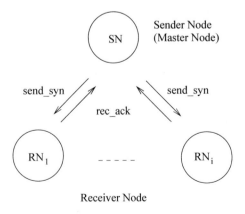

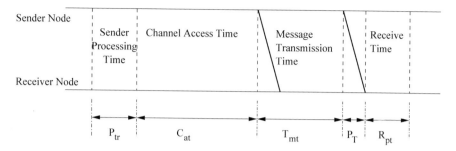

Fig. 5.2 Message transmission delay from sender node to receiver node

Each sensor node can be either in a sleep or wake mode and this state of the node can change at any time.

The total delivery time of DQTSM is divided into different parts as shown in Fig. 5.2, which directly influences the minimum achievable synchronization error. The main sources of synchronization error come from the medium access, which is random in nature. The MAC layer introduces a random delay that is channel access time C_{at}, sender processing time P_{tr}, and receiver processing time R_{pt}.

DQTSM chooses a Sender Node (SN) as Master Node that transmits messages to synchronize all the sensor nodes in a one-hop wireless network; the Receiver Nodes (RN_i) calculate their received time plus transfer time delay. All the receiving nodes send the *rec_ack* message at different times in order to avoid collisions after receiving the *send_syn* time synchronization message from the sender node. The transmission time and receive time are predictable from the speed of radio signal and size of the transmitted message. The transmit time depends on speed and number of data bits. The receiver node time is calculated using receiver's local timestamps. The calculated accuracy depends on the resolution of the local clock timestamps.

The proposed DQTSM requires only one radio signal strength to synchronize all sensor nodes within a single-hop transmission range. It is fully distributed and effective for both one-hop and multi-hop dense sensor networks, which synchronizes sensor nodes relative to a specific event. It involves fewer synchronization messages in comparison with the other time synchronization protocols, they improve the accuracy of clocks and are more energy-efficient.

5.4 Mathematical Model

The DQTSM protocol is designed for local time message exchange among two or more sensor nodes in WSNs. The Notations are defined in Table 5.1. The message exchange can use MAC layer timestamped frames. The delay between two nodes is the time data made by the sender node and the receiver node. In WSNs, the sender node and the receiver node synchronize with each other when processing the time

Table 5.1 Basic notations

Symbols	Meaning
P_T	Propagation delay
D_T	Total delay
E_T	Estimated time
M	Number of bits
τ	Time to transmit a bit
P_{tr}	Time of transmission processing
C_{at}	Time of channel access
T_{mac}	Time of overall MAC delay
T_{mt}	Time period of synchronization message
R_T	Time of local time of receiver node
R_{pt}	Time of receiver processing
EN_{RE}	Energy consumption of receiver node
EN_{SE}	Energy consumption of sender node
EN_{RP}	Energy consumption of radio signal
EN_P	Energy consumed by the processor
T_{RON}	Time period of radio on
T_{ROFF}	Time period of radio off

message; it then measures both the message transfer period and receiving device processing delay. The receiver node measures the arrival time of the message with reference to the clock of the sender node. P_T is the delay in propagation involving receiver and sender nodes. The Fig. 5.2 shows that message transmission delay from sender node to receiver node of DQTSM, the total delay D_T can be measured as

$$D_T = P_T + E_T + T_{mac} \tag{5.1}$$

where E_T is the estimated time to transmit the signal and can be calculated as

$$E_T = M * \tau \tag{5.2}$$

where M is the amount of bits to transmit and τ is the time to transmit one bit over radio. During frame formation at the MAC layer, local time at a sender node is clocked and formed into a frame. The total delay between the receiver and the sender nodes can be replaced by timestamped frames. The MAC layer introduces a random delay that is channel access time C_{at}, sender processing time P_{tr}, and receiver processing time R_{pt}. The total MAC delay (T_{mac}) is $P_{tr} + C_{at} + R_{pt}$ are from the outcome of delays introduced by several individual random processes. In the proposed protocol, a time synchronization sender sensor node sends a time synchronization message with its time period T_{mt}, which is added after MAC delay and a clear channel is detected. The receiver node calculates its local time R_T.

$$R_T = T_{mt} + P_{tr} + C_{at} + R_{pt} \tag{5.3}$$

The receiver node is then synchronized with the sender node. In WSNs, a receiver node radio signal can synchronize with a sender node with accuracy in terms of micro second. Only one period radio signal transfer is required in the proposed protocol to synchronize all nodes within one-hop in WSNs.

5.4.1 Energy Consumption

In this section, we present energy-efficient time synchronization model for the proposed protocol for WSNs. Consumption of energy by a sensor node in WSNs is essentially due to two main reasons: (i) Radio Signal and (ii) Processor. During active times, the available energy is utilized by processor and radio that depends on the sensor node of their mentioned absolute maximum rating values. EN_{sleep}, is the energy consumption of the nodes during sleep and T_{sleep} is the sleep time. In general, at any particular instant, energy consumption (EN_I) is given by

$$EN_I = EN_{RE} + EN_{SE} + EN_{RP} \tag{5.4}$$

where EN_{RE} and EN_{SE} are energy consumption of receiver and sender node, respectively, and EN_{RP} is the energy consumption of radio signal process. Let EN_P be the Energy consumed by the processor of the node and it is obtained as follows:

$$EN_P = EN_{RP}[T_{RON} + T_{ROFF}] + EN_{sleep} * T_{sleep} \tag{5.5}$$

The total energy consumed (EN_{Total}) by a node at any instant of time is given by

$$EN_{Total} = EN_P + EN_I \tag{5.6}$$

5.4.2 DQTSM Algorithm

The aim is to design a DQTSM protocol that attains exact and efficient network wide synchronization by reducing the sources of synchronization error. The master node is in control of synchronizing its direct neighbors through the messages. The receiving sensor nodes need to send the response at different times to avoid collisions after receiving the time synchronization message from the Master node. Prior work TTS [21] protocol divides the synchronization hops, limited to small networking area, results in increased synchronization error. The protocol FTSP [8] has a high synchronization error because the nodes are synchronized with the root node and need more synchronization messages. The Algorithm 5.1 details the Distributed Qos in Time Synchronized MAC Protocol.

Algorithm 5.1: Distributed Qos in Time Synchronized Mac Protocol (DQTSM)

---

1 Initialize N number of sensor nodes;
2 Select the sender node as the Master-Node;
3 Receiver-Node → Send-Syn;
4 Receiver-Node → Rec-Ack (MasterNode); //Receiver node sends ACK to the Master node
    after the time Synchronization message
5 Receiver-Node ↔ Sender-Node; //Message Exchange
6 Receiver-Node calculates its local time; //Minimizes Synchronization error
7 Receiver-Node = R_T; // Local time Set
8 **return**;

5.5   Performance Evaluation

In this part, we compare the performance of DQTSM protocol with FTSP [8] and TTS
[21] and time synchronization protocols. The performance evaluation parameters in
ns-2 [22] are: Energy consumption, Synchronization messages, and Synchronization
error time. In this simulation, hundred nodes are arbitrarily deployed in a square
shaped region in the area of 600 × 600 m with clock rates and initial clock values
randomly assigned. Each node has a fixed transmission range of 250 m and the
simulation time is set to 700 s.

Figure 5.3 shows that synchronization error enhances with the number of sensor
nodes in a 600m × 600m area, to keep the error in the range of microseconds. The
number of nodes is varied from 10 to 100. The DQTSM protocol achieves two times
better performance than TTS as account of time-stamping the signal messages in the

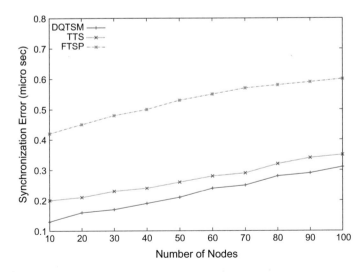

Fig. 5.3 Synchronization error with increase in number of nodes

Medium Access Control. Synchronization error comes from the non-deterministic random time delay for a message transfer between two nodes, which is typically a few microseconds.

To measure the simulation performance metrics of the DQTSM, FTSP, and TTS the number of synchronization messages and the number of sensor nodes are considered. Figure 5.4 shows the result of a number of synchronization messages with the number of sensor nodes for various time synchronization protocols. The number of synchronization messages sent by TTS and FTSP is more compared to our proposed DQTSM protocol, where the Master node is responsible for synchronizing its direct neighbors with a minimum number of synchronization messages. In Fig. 5.4, the TTS scheme exchanges 1200 messages between sensor nodes and our proposed scheme requires just 800 message exchanges.

Figure 5.5 shows that energy consumption in FTSP is more dependent on the density of sensor nodes. In contrast, DQTSM and TTS are less affected by the number of sensor nodes in the wireless network. When the number of nodes increases from 10 to 100, DQTSM becomes more energy-efficient, i.e., 37.5% more than FTSP and TTS. This is because each node in the network is either in a sleep/wake state and a node can change its state at any time. The nodes use minimum communication messages for the synchronization of the sensor nodes. The combined effect of low synchronization error and lower number of synchronization messages reduces the consumption of energy resulting in an increased lifetime of the Wireless Sensor Network.

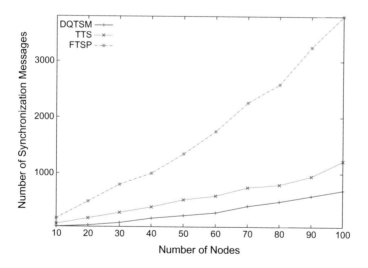

Fig. 5.4 Number of synchronization message with number of nodes

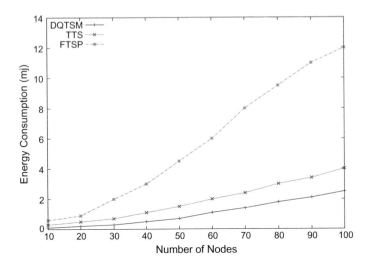

Fig. 5.5   Energy consumption of different synchronization protocol

5.6   Summary

In this work, we have designed DQTSM protocol to reduce the time synchronization of the entire network with minimum messages overhead for WSNs. The DQTSM achieves stability in maintaining clock accuracy at the same time. The combined effect of low error and low synchronization messages decrease the consumption of energy resulting in an increased life span of WSNs.

References

1. M. Mock, R. Frings, E. Nett, S. Trikaliotis, Continuous clock synchronization in wireless real-time applications, in *Proceedings of 19th IEEE Symposium on Reliable Distributed Systems* (2000), pp. 125–133
2. J. Elson, L. Girod and D. Estrin, Fine-grained network time synchronization using reference broadcasts, in *Proceedings of the Fifth Symposium on Operating Systems Design and Implementation (OSDI 2002)* (2002), pp. 147–163
3. S. Ganeriwal, R. Kumar, M.B. Srivastava, Timing-sync protocol for sensor networks, in *Proceedings of the ACM Conference on Networked Sensor Systems (SenSys)* (2003), pp. 138–149
4. J.V. Greunen, J. Rabaey, Lightweight Time Synchronization for Sensor Networks, in *Proceedings of the 2nd ACM International Conference on Wireless Sensor Networks and Applications (WSNA)* (2003), pp. 11–19
5. H. Dai, R. Han, Tsync: a lightweight bidirectional time synchronization service for wireless sensor networks. ACM SIGMOBILE Mob. Comput. Commun. Rev. **8**(1), 125–139 (2004)
6. Q. Gao, K.J. Blow, D.J. Holding, Simple algorithm for improving time synchronization in WSNs. IEEE Electron. Lett. **40**(14), 889–891 (2004)
7. S.C. Visweswara, A.A. Goel, R. Dutta, An adaptive ad-hoc self-organizing scheduling for quasi-periodic sensor traffic, in *IEEE SECON* (2004), pp. 342–351

8. M. Maroti, B. Kusy, G. Simon, A. Ledeczi, The flooding time synchronization protocol, in *Proceedings of the 2nd ACM International Conference on Embedded Networked Sensor Systems* (2004), pp. 39–49

9. W. Ye, F. Silva, J. Heidemann, Ultra-low duty cycle MAC with scheduled channel polling, Technical Report ISI-TR-604, USC Information Sciences Institute (2005)

10. S. Ganeriwal, D. Ganesan, H. Sim, V. Tsiatsis, M.B. Srivastava, Estimating clock uncertainty for efficient duty-cycling in sensor networks, in *3rd ACM Conference on Embedded Networked Sensor Systems (SenSys)*, (San Diego, California, 2005), pp. 130–141

11. W. Su, I.F. Akyildiz, Time-diffusion synchronization protocol for wireless sensor networks. IEEE/ACM Trans. Netw. **13**(2), 384–397 (2005)

12. Q. Li, D. Rus, Global clock synchronization in sensor network. IEEE Trans. Comput. **55**(2), 214–226 (2006)

13. O. Younis, S. Fahmy, Distributed clustering in ad hoc sensor networks: a hybrid, energy-efficient approach. IEEE Trans. Mob. Comput. **5**(10), 1471–1472 (2006)

14. K.L. Noh, Q. Chaudhari, E. Serpedin, B. Suter, Novel clock phase offset and skew estimation using two-way timing message exchanges for wireless sensor networks. IEEE Trans. Commun. **4**, 766–777 (2007)

15. Y. Jia, L. Zhao, B. Ma, A hierarchical clustering-based routing protocol for wireless sensor networks supporting multiple data aggregation qualities. Int. J. Sens. Netw. **4**(1), 79–91 (2008)

16. L. Li, Y. Liu, H. Yang, H. Wang, A precision adaptive average time synchronization protocol in wireless sensor networks, in *IEEE International Conference on Information and Automation (ICIA)* (2008), pp. 65–70

17. B.K. Kim, S. Hong, K. Hur, D. Eom, Energy-efficient and rapid time synchronization for wireless sensor networks. IEEE Trans. Consum. Electron. **56**(4), 2258–2266 (2010)

18. R. Albu, Y. Labit, T. Gayraud, P. Berthou, *An Energy-Efficient Clock Synchronization Protocol for Wireless Sensor Networks* (In Wireless Days, IFIP, 2010), pp. 1–5

19. Y.C. Wu, Q. Chaudhari, E. Serpedian, Clock synchronization of wireless sensor networks. IEEE Signal Process. Mag. **28**(1), 124–138 (2011)

20. Y. Wu, S. Fahmy, N.B. Shroff, Optimal sleep/wake scheduling for time-synchronized sensor networks with QoS guarantees. IEEE/ACM Trans. Netw. **17**(5), 1508–1521 (2009)

21. J. Wang, S. Zhang, D. Gao, Y. Wang, Two-hop Time Synchronization Protocol for Sensor Networks. EURASIP J. Wirel. Commun. Netw. Springer, pp. 1–10 (2014)

22. ns-2 Simulator, http://www.isi.edu/nsnam/ns/

Chapter 6
ERRAP: Efficient Retransmission Qos-Aware MAC Scheme for WSNs

Abstract In this chapter, we have proposed an Efficient Retransmission Random Access Protocol (ERRAP) that retransmits a new frame within a pre-calculated time slot, which combines scheme of collision avoidance and energy management for low-cost, short-range wireless radios, and low-energy sensor applications. This scheme focuses on efficient MAC scheme to provide autonomous Quality of Service (QoS) to the sensor nodes in one-hop QoS retransmission group in WSNs. The sensor nodes join the network only during random access time. The time interval between random access period could be small. Our simulation results demonstrate the performance of ERRAP protocol which increases the delivery probability and reduces the energy consumption.

6.1   Introduction

Optimal retransmission is the process of sending frames to the sink multiple numbers of times to achieve the maximum delivery probability. Optimal retransmission in WSNs is mainly focused on QoS in provisioning data frame delivery probability and energy efficiency. The network topology consists of a large number of source nodes which are distributed and decentralized in one-hop communication range. The throughput requirements are low because the source collects and transmits the data to the sink.

6.2   Related Works

Retransmission mechanism has been adopted as one of the most popular techniques for improving transmission reliability in WSNs. Message transmission in WSNs is unreliable due to several factors such as the unreliability of wireless links,

---

Reprinted by permission from Springer Nature: Springer LNEE-284, M. Kumaraswamy, K. Shaila, V. Tejaswi, K. R. Venugopal, S. S. Iyengar, L. M. Patnaik, Efficient Retransmission QoS-Aware MAC Scheme in Wireless Sensor Networks, NetCom'13, Copyright (2013).

interference from hostile environments. Pai et al. [1] design a novel adaptive retransmission algorithm to improve the misclassification probability of distributed detection with error-correcting codes in fault tolerant classification system for Wireless Sensor Networks. The local decision of each sensor is based on its detection result. The detection result must be transmitted to a fusion center to make a final decision.

Lu et al. [2] propose a MAC layer cooperative retransmission mechanism and a node can retransmit lost packets on behalf of its neighboring node. However, although each lost packet can be recovered by a neighboring node, it still requires a new transmission for each retransmission attempt, which largely limits its ability to increase the throughput of the network. Cerutti et al. [3] propose fixed Time-Division Multiple-Access (TDMA) scheme delivery. When a node overhears a neighbor's unsuccessful packet, it may retransmit that packet in its own allocated slot, provided the queue of its own packets is empty. Dianati et al. [4] present concurrent cooperation communication among the nodes to retransmit a packet to the destination if they receive the corresponding negative acknowledgment from the destination.

Xiong et al. [5] consider cooperative forwarding in WSNs from a MAC layer perspective, which means a receiver can only decode one transmission at a time. Fan et al. [6] propose an interesting MAC layer any casting mechanism and randomized waiting at the application layer, to facilitate data aggregation spatially and temporally in structure-free sensor networks. They address the collision problem by proposing a modified CSMA/CA protocol and randomized waiting scheme to reduce the number of retransmissions. Noh et al. [7] propose Active Caching (AC) to achieve desired Communication Reliability (CR) levels of the various sensor network applications. This is a flexible loss recovery mechanism, when the packet delivery rate during multi-hop transmission from a source to an intermediate node decreases below the CR, AC retransmits lost packets from the source node to the intermediate node so that the intermediate node has all data packets just like the source node.

Qureshi et al. [8] propose a latency and bandwidth efficient coding algorithm based on the principles of network coding for retransmitting lost packets in a single-hop wireless multicast network and demonstrate its effectiveness over previously proposed network coding based retransmission algorithms. Aggelos et al. [9] present a time-offset based distributed relay selection strategy where the relay node with excellent channel quality has the smallest time value. The other node relays hear the transmission and withdraw from competition to transmit. He et al. [10] propose the single-relay Cooperative Automatic Repeat Request (CARQ) protocol. In CARQ, the best relay node is selected in a distributed manner by using a different back-off time before packet retransmission. In a dense network, due to high possible collision probability among different contending relays, an optimized relay selection scheme is introduced to maximize system energy efficiency by reducing collision probability.

Chu et al. [11] present relay selection and selection diversity for coded cooperation in Wireless Sensor Networks, with complexity attribute for the sensor nodes. In earlier methods, a relaying technique based on Repeat-Accumulate (RA) codes is introduced, where the relay does not carry out decoding and simply uses demodulated bits to form code words. Suriyachai et al. [12] provide deterministic bounds for reliability and node-to-node delay. It is based on collision-free TDMA consisting of fixed-length slots called epochs about its channel requirements. It consumes low energy. Ruiz et al. [13] propose an architecture collaboration in which the Medium Access Control and routing protocols discover and preserve routes and organize sensor nodes into clusters and to schedule the access to the transmission medium in a coordinated time-shared approach. It achieves QoS and reduces energy consumption by avoiding collisions and considerably lowering idle listening.

Tannious et al. [14] present the secondary node user that exploits the retransmissions of primary node user packets in order to achieve a higher transmission rate. The secondary node receiver can potentially decode the primary node users packet in the first transmission. Bai et al. [15] propose a design of IEEE 802.11 based wireless network for MAC that dynamically adjusts the retransmission limit to track the optimal trade-off between transmission delay and packet losses to optimize the overall network control system performance. Volkhausen et al. [16] focus on cooperative relaying; it exploits temporal and spatial diversity by additionally transmitting via a relay node; such relaying improves packet error rates and transmits only once rather than on each individual hop along the routing path. This cooperation reduces the total number of transmissions and improves overall performance.

Levorato et al. [17] propose the optimal throughput which is achieved by the secondary node users in wireless networks when the primary node user adopts a retransmission-based error control scheme. The secondary node users maximize the throughput, with a constraint on the performance loss and an increased failure probability of the primary node user. Wang et al. [18] propose the local cooperative relay for opportunistic data transmitting in mobile ad-hoc networks. The local cooperative relay selects the best local relay node without additional overhead; such real-time selection can effectively bridge the broken links in mobile networks and maintain a robust topology.

Sudhaakar et al. [19] propose a novel Medium Access Control scheme for a dense WSNs, that are in single to the one or more sink nodes. The source nodes have only the transmitter that reduces the hardware consumption of energy. These nodes cannot receive any signals like ACK/NAK. The sensor nodes transmit usually small data frames to the sink nodes occasionally and therefore their throughput requirement is low. The sink nodes are the only nodes in the wireless network that have receiver modules and can receive the transmissions of the sensor nodes.

6.3 System Model and Problem Definition

Let a WSN consist of N nodes as shown in Fig. 6.1, having source nodes and one or two sink nodes. In WSNs, each sensor node is in single-hop transmission range of the sink node. The event sensed source node transmit data frame by choosing a variable slot arbitrarily. The nodes can join the wireless network only during the random access periods. The time interval between random access periods could be small. The nodes randomly decide whether they should retransmit to help the

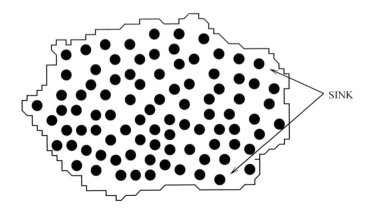

Fig. 6.1 Nodes deployment in wireless sensor network

frame delivery depending on some predefined optimal retransmission probabilities. The sink node receives exactly one error-free transmission frame in a slot, without collision with other simultaneous transmissions. The main objectives of the proposed work are to

(i) Maximize the data delivery probability of the sensor nodes in the QoS groups.
(ii) Minimize the number of frame retransmissions in the network, this reduces the consumption of energy of sensor nodes and maximizes the frame delivery probability.
(iii) Guarantee that the sent frame is received at the sink.

The assumptions are

(i) All nodes are homogeneous.
(ii) The sensor nodes are arbitrarily distributed within a region.
(iii) Frame generated at each node follows a Poisson distribution.
(iv) Only one wide channel is available for all communicating nodes.

The ERRAP provides QoS to the nodes using random access mode where each node depending on local conditions transmits data frame by selecting a variable slot randomly. The objective is to develop a decentralized MAC protocol to provide QoS guarantees for both time-critical and non time-critical sensor applications. The most important metrics to analyze the QoS performance of MAC protocol is frame delivery probability and energy efficiency.

In WSNs, each sensor node data frame transmission duration is relatively small when compared to the data frame that is generated at a constant rate, i.e., one frame every T units of time. In addition, if a frame cannot be successfully delivered within T units of time, the data frames are simply neglected. This makes sure that the new data frames have a greater chance of being successfully delivered. Thus, the maximum delivery probability that can be achieved by each individual sensor node increases eventually, so that all the sensor nodes in the WSNs achieve their required Quality of Service in terms of data delivery probability.

In addition, we consider a WSNs architecture in which the source nodes generate data and transmit periodically to the sink node. The set of N nodes are partitioned into two QoS groups C_1 and C_2, with each group containing m_1 and m_2 nodes, respectively. The frame transmission duration T_{fr} of all nodes are assumed to be the same. Each node in C_1 and C_2 requires minimum frame delivery probability q ($1 < j < 2$). The protocol ERRAP calculates the optimal number of retransmissions y_k for each C_k, such that, if every sensor node in C_k transmits y_k times in every T_{fr} units of time, it should achieve a delivery probability of at least q.

6.4 Mathematical Model

6.4.1 One-Hop Retransmissions

We have assumed that the source nodes generate data at constant rate of one frame every T units of time and the retransmission time for each frame is much smaller than the duration of frame transmission T_{fr}, to achieve equal frame delivery probability by all the nodes in the WSNs. Under this assumption, the frame arrival rate can be modeled as a Poisson distribution. The quantity of sensor nodes in the wireless network is denoted by N and the number of retransmissions by each node for each frame is denoted by y_k. The notations are defined in Table 6.1.

The frame arrival rate at the source nodes can be modeled as a Poisson distribution and the probability that p frames are transmitted in an interval T_t with $Q(N)$ the probability of N arrivals in one time slot is given by

$$Q(N) = (\beta T_t)/p! e^{-\beta T_t} \tag{6.1}$$

	Symbols	Meaning
Table 6.1 List of symbols used	N	Total number of sensor nodes
	T	Data frame generation time
	C_k	Number of QoS group
	m_k	Number of nodes in each group
	T_{fr}	Duration of frame transmission
	y_k	Number of retransmission
	B	Frame arrival rate
	P	Number of frames
	Q	Frame delivery probability
	q_k	Minimum delivery probability
	t_g	Overall traffic generated by all nodes
	T_t	Time of p frame transmission
	cs	Carrier sense period of frame
	t_k	Time of retransmission in C_k

where β is the rate of traffic generated by all other sensor nodes inside the transmission range of a node and is equal to $(N-1)/T * y$.

The probability that the frame transmitted by node k does not collide, so it is same as the probability that no frames were transmitted by the other $(N-1)$ sensor nodes in an interval $2T_{fr}$. Therefore Q_{nc} is

$$Q_{nc} = e^{-\beta T_{fr}} \tag{6.2}$$

The above discussion presents the probability that a frame transmitted by node k is successfully received by the sink. However, node k transmits y_k copies of the frame at random instants in every time interval T_{fr}. Hence the actual parameter of interest is the probability that at least one of these y_k copies is successfully received at the sink, which is defined as the QoS delivery probability of the node. The $Q(y_c)$, the collision probability of each frame is given by

$$Q(y_c) = (1 - Q_{nc})^y \tag{6.3}$$

The probability of successful transmission of sensor data frame $Q(y_s)$ is given by

$$Q(y_s) = (1 - Q(y_c)) \tag{6.4}$$

Combining the above equations, we have

$$Q(y_s) = (1 - Q(y_c)) \tag{6.5}$$

$$Q(y_s) = 1 - (1 - Q_{nc})^y \tag{6.6}$$

$$Q(y) = Q(y_s) = 1 - (1 - e^{-2\beta T_{fr}})^y \tag{6.7}$$

The $Q(y)$ expresses the QoS delivery probability as function of the number of retransmissions attempted by each node in the interval T_{fr}. The maximum frame delivery probability Q_{max} that can be achieved is given by

$$Q(y) = Q(y_s) = Q_{max} = 1 - (1 - e^{-2\beta T_{fr}})^y \tag{6.8}$$

The above result gives the relationship between the maximum frame delivery probabilities that can be achieved, the number of retransmission attempts that each sensor node makes in every interval T_{fr}.

6.4.2 Two QoS Groups

Consider delivery probability of two QoS groups C_1 and C_2 containing m_1 and m_2 nodes and requiring minimum frame delivery probability q. Number of nodes in C_k

is m_k and each node in C_k retransmits y_k times in every interval t_k. The number of retransmissions y_k is the same for all the nodes in C_k.

The analysis is similar to that of one-hop retransmission, the probability of transmission from the node in C_k that does not collide with transmission from any other node in the network and is given by

$$Q_{nc}(j) = e^{-2\beta t_g(\tau_{cs}+T_{fr})} \tag{6.9}$$

where β_{tg} is distinct as the overall traffic produced by all nodes inside the transmission range of a node and its rate is given by

$$\beta_{tg} = \sum m_k y_k / t_k \tag{6.10}$$

The successful frame delivery probability achieved by node in C_k can be evaluated as

$$Q_{suc}(k) = 1 - (1 - e^{-2\beta t_g(\tau_{cs}+T_{fr})})^{y_k+1} \tag{6.11}$$

where τ_{cs} is the carrier sense period and T_{fr} is the duration of a frame transmission.

6.4.3 ERRAP Algorithm

The purpose of the ERRAP algorithm is to get the optimal retransmission value between y_{low} and y_{high} that minimizes the total sensor network traffic and each node in WSNs achieves maximum delivery probability in the background traffic. There are two QoS groups, consisting of C_1, C_2 containing m_1, m_2 nodes and requiring minimum delivery probability of q.

In this section, the performance of retransmission algorithm ERRAP is discussed to find the solution to the optimization problem in one-hop QoS group containing N nodes and also supports TWO QoS group as shown in Algorithm 6.1. The purpose of the ERRAP algorithm is to get the optimal retransmission value between y_{low} and y_{high} that minimizes the total sensor network traffic and each node in the network achieves maximum delivery probability and with minimal energy consumption.

6.5 Performance Evaluation

6.5.1 Simulation Setup

The performance of ERRAP has been evaluated using *ns-2* simulator package with respect to frame delivery probability and energy consumption. A random flat-grid scenario is chosen for deployment of the nodes within 230m × 230m area. Two-

---

Algorithm 6.1: Efficient Retransmission QoS-Aware MAC Algorithm (ERRAP)

---

1 Each source node (Ni) transmits y copies at random instant;
2 For Minimum Number of Retransmission from each QoS Group;
3 **for** *each* $y_k \in y_{low}$ *to* y_{high} **do**
4      $Q_{suc}(k) = Q(y) = 1 - (1 - e^{-2\beta T_{fr}})y_k$;
5   **if** $Q(y) \geq q$ **then**
6   Success True;
7   **else**
8   No feasible solution exits;
9   **return** y;

---

ray ground indication model for radio propagation and omnidirectional antenna is utilized. The transmission bandwidth is set to 50 Mbps. For One-hop retransmission and Two QoS groups, it is assumed that the number of nodes N is 100, data arrival rate T = 1ms and frame transmission time $T_p = 6.4 \times 10^{-4}$ ms.

6.5.2 One-Hop QoS Group

The results for $Q(y)$ given in Eq. 6.8 for one-hop retransmission, consisting of N = 100 nodes is plotted in Fig. 6.2. It shows that the probability of the delivery of frames initially increases with the number of retransmissions, reaches maximum and then decreases. The simulation and numerical analysis results show that the maximum delivery probability of $Q(y)$ is 0.9990 for 50m × 50m area when y = 4 or y = 5. The minimum delivery probability $Q(y)$ is 0.978 is achieved for $3 \leq y \leq 9$. The ERRAP scheme minimizes the network traffic when y = 3 and maximizes the probability of delivery of data frames when the retransmission value y = 4.

The second set of curves of ERRAP of simulation results is comparable with the theoretical analysis. The delivery probability $Q(y)$ is 0.96 when the sensor nodes are randomly distributed in 230 m × 230 m region. Since the simulation performance of sensor nodes is poor in a large region, we assume that the frame loss is only due to channel errors and not due to collisions or interference.

Figure 6.2 illustrates that the number of retransmission by each sensor node is reduced by choosing the value for y as 3 or 4. This increases the probability of frame delivery, which in turn increases the lifetime of the sensor nodes.

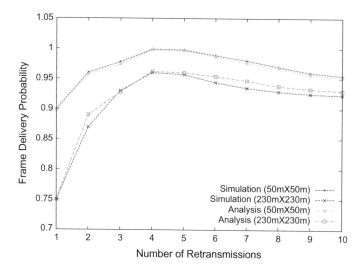

Fig. 6.2 Frame delivery probability of one-hop retransmission simulation and analysis result for ERRAP

6.5.3 Two QoS Groups

For analysis and simulation, we assume that there are only two QoS groups. The delivery probability of two QoS groups are C_1 and C_2 consisting of m_1 and m_2 nodes and requiring minimum delivery probability q.

Figure 6.3 shows the simulation and numerical analysis for maximizing the delivery probability. The delivery probability $Q(y)$ is high for small sized networks, say, for nodes $m_1 = 30$, $m_2 = 30$, and $Q(y)$ is 0.9999. For $m_2 = 80$ and a smaller value of $m_1 = 30$, $Q(y)$ is 0.9998. Similarly, with a large number of nodes $m_1 = m_2 = 80$, the delivery probability $Q(y)$ drops to nearly 0.9996. It is observed that the delivery probability $Q(y)$ depends on the number of sensor nodes in each QoS groups.

6.5.4 Minimizing Energy Consumption

ERRAP protocol minimizes the consumption of energy between the source nodes and the sink node. The lifetime of sensor nodes in the wireless network is directly proportional to the energy dissipation of each node. The consumed energy in sensors includes the energy required for sensing, transmitting, receiving, and processing of data. ERRAP protocol contributes to energy efficiency by minimizing collisions and retransmissions.

Figure 6.4 depicts the average consumption of energy of the ERRAP scheme for different values of retransmissions for 2 K data frame when the aggregated data rate

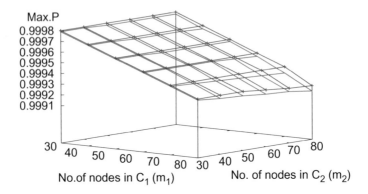

Fig. 6.3 Analysis and simulation results of maximum probability (Max. P) for two QoS groups

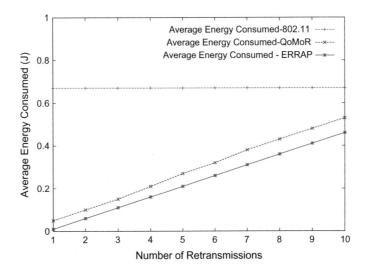

Fig. 6.4 Average energy consumption

generated by all the nodes is about 50Mbps. The energy consumed by the ERRAP scheme for the number of retransmissions value 10, is less than the energy consumed by the QoMoR and 802.11b protocol. The ERRAP protocol uses shorter frame slots, avoiding control frame like RTS and CTS, which unnecessarily consume bandwidth and energy. ERRAP consumes 9.4% lower energy than QoMoR and 28.36% lower than 802.11b.

Figure 6.5 depicts the frame delivery probabilities achieved by ERRAP, QoMoR, and 802.11b. The frame delivery probability of ERRAP algorithm is significantly higher than that achieved by the QoMoR and 802.11b protocols. Both QoMoR and 802.11b do not use the available bandwidth as efficiently as ERRAP. The ERRAP provides QoS to the nodes using arbitrary access mode where each sensor node

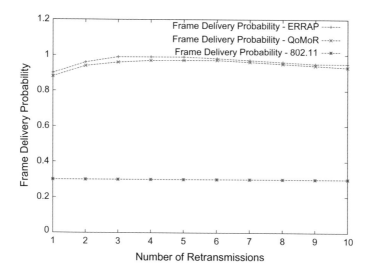

Fig. 6.5 Frame delivery probability of ERRAP, QoMoR, and 802.11b

transmits data frame by choosing variable slots randomly according to the participating number of sensor nodes; each node takes local decisions, depending on some
predefined efficient retransmission probabilities.

When the number of sensor nodes is large and the aggregate data rate matches
the available bandwidth, the performance of the ERRAP algorithm is significantly
better than QoMoR and 802.11b both in terms of Quality of Service, frame delivery
probability and consumption of energy. ERRAP is 3.13% better that QoMoR and
802.11b.

6.6 Summary

We have implemented an Efficient Retransmission Random Access Protocol
(ERRAP), which combines Collision Avoidance (CA) and efficient energy management QoS-Aware MAC protocol for WSNs. A mathematical model is designed
to evaluate the maximum frames delivery probability and minimize the energy consumption by optimal retransmission technique. In the ERRAP protocol, each source
node simply retransmits each of its data frame an optimal number of times within a
given period of time in one-hop QoS group and Two QoS groups. Simulation results
show that each source node employs probabilistic retransmission to minimize the
energy consumption and maximize the frame delivery probability.

References

1. H. Pai, J. Sung, Y.S. Han, Adaptive retransmission for distributed detection in wireless sensor networks, in *IEEE International Conference on Sensor Networks, Ubiquitous and Trustworthy Computing*, vol. 2 (2006), p. 27
2. K. Lu, S. Fu, Y. Qian, Increasing the throughput of wireless LANs via cooperative retransmission. IEEE Proc. Globecom 5231–5235 (2007)
3. I. Cerutti, A. Fumagalli, G. Ho, Saturation throughput gain in fixed multiplexing radio networks with cooperative retransmission protocols, in *Proceedings IEEE International Conference on Communications (ICC)*, vol. 10 (2006), pp. 4489–4494
4. M. Dianati, X. Ling, S. Naik, X. Shen, A node cooperative ARQ scheme for wireless ad-hoc networks. IEEE Trans. Veh. Technol. **55**(3), 1032–1044 (2006)
5. L. Xiong, L. Libman, G. Mao, Optimal strategies for cooperative Mac-layer retransmission in wireless networks, in *Proceedings IEEE Wireless Communication and Networking Conference* (2008), pp. 1495–1500
6. K.W. Fan, S. Liu, P. Sinha, Structure-free data aggregation in sensor networks. IEEE Trans. Mob. Comput. **6**, 929942 (2007)
7. S. Noh, E. Lee, S. Oh, T. Lee, S. Kim, Effective retransmission scheme for supporting communication reliability in sensor networks. IEEE Pers. Indoor Mob. Radio Commun. 2180–2185 (2010)
8. J. Qureshi, C.H. Foh, J. Cai, An efficient network coding based retransmission algorithm for wireless multicast. IEEE Pers. Indoor Mob. Radio Commun. 691–695 (2009)
9. B. Aggelos, K. Ashish, P.R. David, L. Andrew, A simple cooperative diversity method based on network path selection. IEEE Sel. Areas Commun. **24**(3), 659672 (2006)
10. X. He, F. Y. Li, An optimal energy efficient cooperative retransmission MAC scheme in wireless networks, in *IEEE International Conference on Wireless Vehicular Technology, Information Theory, Aerospace and Electronic System Technology*, p. 15 (2011)
11. J.P.K. Chu, R.S. Adve, A.W. Eckford, Relay selection for low-complexity coded cooperation, in *IEEE Global Electronics Communications Conference*, pp. 1008–1012 (2007)
12. P. Suriyachai, U. Roedig, A. Scott, Implementation of A MAC protocol for QoS support in wireless sensor networks, in *Proceedings of the IEEE International Conference on Pervasive Computing and Communications*, p. 16 (2009)
13. J. Ruiz, J. Gallardo, L. Villasenor Gonzalez, D. Makrakis, H. Mouftah, QUATTRO: QoS-capable cross-layer MAC protocol for wireless sensor networks, in *IEEE Global Telecommunications Conference*, p. 16 (2009)
14. R.A. Tannious, A. Nosratinia, Cognitive radio protocols based on exploiting hybrid ARQ retransmissions. IEEE Trans. Wirel. Commun. **9**(9), 28332841 (2010)
15. J. Bai, E.P. Eyisi, Y. Xue, X.D. Koutsoukos, Dynamic tuning retransmission limit of IEEE 802.11 MAC protocol for networked control systems, in *Proceedings of 3rd IEEE/ACM International Conference on Cyber, Physical and Social Computing (CPSCom)* (2010), pp. 666–671
16. T. Volkhausen, K. Dridger, H.S. Lichte, H. Karl, Efficient cooperative relaying in wireless multi-hop networks with commodity WiFi hardware, in *Proceedings of 10th IEEE International Symposium on Modeling and Optimization in Mobile, Ad Hoc and Wireless Networks(WiOpt)* (2012), pp. 299–304
17. M. Levorato, U. Mitra, M. Zorzi, Cognitive Interference management in retransmission-based wireless networks. IEEE Trans. Inf. Theory **58**(5), 30233046 (2012)
18. Z. Wang, C. Li, Y. Chen, Local cooperative relay for opportunistic data forwarding in mobile ad-hoc networks, in *Proceedings of IEEE International Conference on Communications (ICC)* (2012), pp. 5381–5386
19. R.S. Sudhaakar, S. Yoon, J. Zhao, C. Qiao, A novel QoS aware MAC scheme using optimal retransmission for wireless networks. IEEE Trans. Wirel. Commun. **8**(5), 2230–2235 (2009)

Chapter 7
CBH-MAC: Contention-Based Hybrid MAC Protocol for WSNs

Abstract It is challenging to design a hybrid MAC scheme for delay aware data traffic in WSNs. The Contention-Based Hybrid MAC (CBH-MAC) protocol is proposed where each sensor node operates the reservation procedure used in cross and chain topology, resulting in energy efficiency, maximizing the packet delivery ratio, minimizing contention around the nodes, and reducing end-to-end delay. The neighboring sensor nodes of the receiver and sender receive their individual reservation control packets. The sender transmits data and receives acknowledgment packets during the adaptive contention-free period. As the reservation packets pass through the sensor along the routing path, the sensor nodes reserve the time slots consecutively in multi-hop. The scheme has significant improvement in the end-to-end latency, packet delivery ratio, and energy efficiency.

7.1 Introduction

Energy is mainly consumed in MAC protocols when the node is just listening and waiting for a packet (since it is multi-hop) to be sent. Traffic in WSNs is very low and is triggered by sensing events which are in the form of bursts. A long delay is highly undesirable for time-sensitive applications such as critical situation monitoring and security surveillance. For handling real-time traffic, WSNs require end-to-end latency within an acceptable range. Gathering the sensed real-time data requires Quality of Service aware Medium Access Control protocol in order to ensure efficient utilization of effective delivery of the gathered data and energy resources of the sensor node.

A hybrid MAC protocols combine two periods, i.e., contention-free and contention-based periods. These MAC protocols reserve time slots during contention-based and sensor nodes transfer data in an assigned slot time using adaptive contention-free access time.

Reprinted by permission from Springer Nature: Springer CCIS-292, Kumaraswamy M., Shaila K., Sivasankari H., Tejaswi V., Venugopal K. R., S. S. Iyengar et al, RCH-MAC Protocol for Multihop QoS in Wireless Sensor Networks, ICIP'12, Copyright (2012).

7.2 Related Works

Multi-hop Cross-layer design facilitates to improve network performance by sharing information among the different layers in the networking protocol stack by message passing to achieve better performance. Cross-layer design significantly improves energy efficiency, because WSNs report data in a wireless manner across multi-hop to a sink node. Dam et al. [1] propose energy efficiency and throughput of S-MAC by introducing adaptive duty cycle that dynamically adjusts the length of active periods according to the traffic load variations. T-MAC is proposed to address the S-MAC nodes not participating in the data exchange. Time-out MAC (T-MAC) protocol is similar to S-MAC, but adaptively shortens the listen period. The main contribution of the Time-out Medium Access Control protocol is its adaptive duty cycle approach. T-MAC is capable of adapting to traffic fluctuations and outperforms S-MAC.

Polastre et al. [2] propose a B-MAC (Berkeley MAC) protocol, which uses an unsynchronized contention-based MAC protocol and long preambles to wake up receivers. In order to reduce the power consumption, B-MAC periodically sleeps and wakes up. The energy and latency performance of B-MAC depends on the preamble length. B-MAC uses the clear channel sensing mechanism to progress the channel utilization. B-MAC has high throughput and energy efficient than T-MAC and S-MAC.

Lu et al. [3] propose low-latency and energy efficient MAC designed for unidirectional data assembly tree. Transmission times are assigned to a set of sensor nodes on a data assembly tree. When a target node receives the slot, all its children can transmit, thus contending over the medium. As slots are successive in the data transmission path, the end-to-end latency is low. The problem in DMAC is that collisions between nodes in the same level of the tree are common.

Ye et al. [4] propose a CSMA/CA-based protocol, which uses periodic listening and sleeping to save energy consumption in WSNs. In order to reduce latency due to the low-duty-cycle operation, adaptive listening is employed to develop the sleep delay.

Chen et al. [5] divide the frame into two slots; each sensor node is assigned one slot for wake up and another slot for transmission. The TDMA-MAC protocol guarantees reliable transmission for all types of traffic.

Rhee et al. [6] present a hybrid MAC protocol which dynamically switches between Time Division Multiple Access and Carrier Sense Multiple Access depending on the level of contention. Zebra-MAC is hybrid MAC protocol designed for WSNs and combines different strengths of CSMA and TDMA protocols. Z-MAC uses the Distributed Randomized (DRAND) algorithm to assign each node a time slot to guarantee that no two-hop neighbors share the same slot. It operates in either a high contention level (HCL) and low contention level (LCL) mode.

Rajendran et al. [7] develop a TDMA-based MAC protocol based on the idea of Neighbor-Aware Contention Resolution. In this approach, each node calculates the priority of its one-hop and two-hop neighbors by applying MD5 hash of the concatenation of the sensor node id and the slot time t. The sensor node with maximum priority is the owner of the slot. Syrotiuk et al. [8] combine TDMA and CSMA/CA to obtain hybrid access scheme that provides good throughput under both low and high traffic loads. First, each node assigns unique time slot in its neighborhood, where each slot is partitioned for sensing and placing data. The owner of the slot initiates the collision avoidance (RTS/CTS) message exchange in the sensing period, where other nodes remain silent and infer whether the slot owner is utilizing the slot or not. If the slot owners have data to transmit, it proceeds with data transmission after successful RTS/CTS handshake. Otherwise, other nodes may utilize this slot after contending for the channel with RTS/CTS handshake.

Sridharan et al. [9] propose algorithm for assigning time slots in multi-hop network called MMF-TDMA. The concurrent transmission works for three or more hops. The algorithm has to be initialized when a new node is assigned a time slot. Mangharam et al. [10] propose TDMA-based protocol that is applicable to networks which require predictability in throughput, latency, and energy consumption. Hardware-based global time synchronization is used. Two phases, namely topology-gathering and scheduling are included in RT-LINK. A cycle is defined as the duration between two synchronization pulses, which consists of a large number of frames divided into two parts: scheduled and contention slots. Each node that wants to transmit data periodically sends Hello messages by randomly selecting slot within the contention slots. A Hello message is transmitted in multi-hop manner to the sink node, which is responsible for network-wide slot assignment. The node is active in its assigned slots.

Chen et al. [11] propose PR-MAC (Path-oriented Real-time MAC protocol) used for monitoring applications where data is sent periodically. A sensor node starts by sending a message to the sink using a contention-based MAC protocol. This message contains description of the sensed value and the path taken by the message. Using the reverse path, the sink nodes send a series of control messages to the relaying nodes, which indicate the periodicity of the subsequent messages that act as resource reservation messages. Once all relaying nodes are contacted, the path is set up and the sink node expects data message to reach it in a real-time fashion.

Watteyne et al. [12] present schedule in a distributed way. It is designed for linear networks. The protocol switches between two modes: unprotected (contention-based) and protected (contention-free). Alarm messages are transmitted in unprotected mode as long as there are no collisions. Each node relays a message when back-off time proportional to its distance to the sink elapses. In case of collision, the protocol switches to protected mode, which avoids collision by channel reservation. Because the unprotected mode allows for faster transmission, the protocol switches back to this mode whenever possible. This protocol does not require synchronization and constructs the schedule in a fully distributed manner.

Kim et al. [13] design a protocol to decrease latency, where reception periods are allocated to each synchronized node on a common channel. The multiple packets on different frequencies are sent to neighbors in a predetermined hopping sequence resulting in bursts of messages that travel across channels, reducing latency. Incel et al. [14] propose a Lightweight MAC (LMAC), TDMA distributed protocol for a two-hop neighborhood and efficient for high delivery network. Du et al. [15] uses a

Pioneer Control Frame (PION) to delivery packets over multi-hops in a single cycle reducing latency and handling traffic contention efficiently.

In recent years, hybrid MAC protocols have been proposed which incorporates the advantages of cooperation of contention-based and TDMA-based MAC protocols. All these protocols divide the access channel into two parts, in which control packets are sent in random access period and data packets are transmitted during the scheduled time. The control channel schedules the data access. Compared to contention-based phase and TDMA-based phase MAC protocols, hybrid protocols gains high-energy savings and offer flexibility.

Wang et al. [16] propose a hybrid MAC (H-MAC) protocol that combines energy-efficient scheme of contention-based and TDMA-based Medium Access Control protocols for WSNs to improve the network performance. H-MAC uses channel reservation method to decrease end-to-end delay by allowing packets to go through multi-hops with a single Medium Access Control frame. It reduces the queuing delay by giving highest priority to channel access and using a short frame format that speeds up packet delivery ratio.

7.3 System Model and Problem Definition

Energy efficiency and end-to-end latency in WSNs are interdependent on each other. A node reserves a time slot during the adaptive contention-free time period and operates the reservation procedure during the contention period. The neighboring sensor nodes of the sender and the receiver accept their individual reservation control packets. The main objectives of our work are to minimize end-to-end transmission delay, improve packet delivery ratio, and minimize the consumption of energy in WSNs. The assumptions are

(i) All the sensor nodes are static and homogeneous.
(ii) Nodes are equipped with omnidirectional antennas.
(iii) Nodes communicate with each other through packets.

It is assumed that nodes are influential devices and every sensor node is synchronized at the initial phase. The frame format of CBH-MAC protocol is divided into three phases, as shown in Fig. 7.1. It consists of (i) sync time (t_{st}), (ii) direct access time (t_{da}) followed by (iii) adaptive contention-free access time (t_{ac}). In this case, a node operates the reservation method during the contention-based phase and reserves a time slot in the adaptive contention-free phase. First, reservation control packets are transmitted by every neighboring sensor nodes of the sender and the receiver accepts their individual reservation control packets. After reservation, the sender transfers data and receives Acknowledgement packets during the adaptive contention-free phase.

The reservation packets take place in sensor nodes along the entire routing path and the sensor nodes are allowed to reserve time slots one after another in multi-hop. The messages are transmitted in the array of RTS/CTS/DATA/ACK sequence

Fig. 7.1 CBH-MAC frame
format

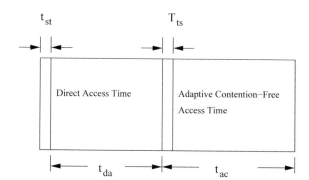

during the contention-based phase by CSMA/CA method. Additionally, the traffic
is transmitted in the same mode as in slotted CSMA/CA when there are free slots
during adaptive contention-free time.

The reservation control packets are allowed in different border spaces and tiny contention window sizes as they are transmitted during contention period. The selected
nodes shall transmit the slot information of the adaptive contention-free time. The slot
information indicates whether the time period is reserved. The adaptive contention-
free phase is divided into 12 time periods. Every source sensor node sends the data,
receives ACK packets in the direction of the reservation procedure. If free slots are
present in adaptive contention-free phase, nodes can compete to acquire the periods
by slotted CSMA/CA method.

On completion of the reservation system, the source node 1 forwards data and
acknowledgs the ACK packet in the reserved period of the adaptive contention-
free time. The slot information is extremely significant for reserving nodes to avoid
collision. In the contention-based time, RTS packets and reservation packets for
transfer sensor data contends for channel acquisition. The protocol gives precedence
to the reservation control packets more than RTS packet.

The H-MAC protocol has long end-to-end delay and QoS cannot be guaranteed,
on account of unstable wireless channel and collisions between the reservation packets as nodes do not maintain neighborhood information. In order to resolve this issue,
designated nodes transfer the slot information during reservation packet transmission. The particular nodes that send or accept the reservation control packets during
contention-based time must transfer the slot information as governed by the random
back-off system. The accurate reservation is maintained between the neighbor nodes.

The adaptive contention-free phase consists of a number of fixed slots. The span
of a time period depends on the traffic load. Each sensor nodes can transmit data
during the free time slots through a slotted CSMA/CA method. Nodes that are not
sending/accepting data can sleep throughout the time periods.

7.4　Mathematical Model

In this section, we analyze the CBH-MAC mathematical model under multi-hop linear chain and cross topology for different traffic flows. Figures 7.2 and 7.3 show the topology for multi-hop transmission. We get both optimal direct access time and adaptive contention-free access time to ensure the lowest end-to-end latency as per traffic load of the sensor network.

Direct access time is a multiple access technique based on CSMA/CA. The time period of this transmission is called the contention window and consists of a predetermined number of transmission slots. The node, which enters back-off, randomly selects a slot in the contention window. It also continuously senses the medium until it selects the contention slot. If it detects transmission from some other node during that time, it enters the back-off state again. If no transmission is detected, it transmits the access packet and captures the medium. In Fig. 7.2, node 1 is a source sensor node that produces data traffic and delivers to sink node 11 through multi-hop transmission. A multi-hop design results in better coverage and reduces power requirement as compared to the single-hop sensor network. In multi-hop Wireless Sensor Network, the sensor nodes self-configure through multi-hop routing to form a network.

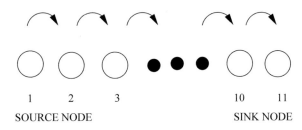

Fig. 7.2　10-hop linear chain topology

SOURCE NODE　　　　　　　　　　　　　　SINK NODE

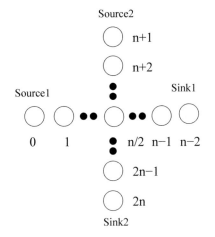

Fig. 7.3　Multi-hop linear cross topology

We assume processing delay, queuing delay, and propagation delay to be negligible at each hop and can be ignored. Efficient scheduling can effectively guarantee quality of service, enable adaptive data rates, and minimize end-to-end latency. We study effective scheduling to achieve these goals with respect to CBH-MAC-based multi-hop sensor networks.

Our objective is to reduce the end-to-end latency from source node 1 to sink node 11. We design a solution to determine the number of time periods in adaptive contention-free access phase and span of the direct access time. Hence, the minimization problem is

$$minimize \quad [End\_to\_End]_{latency} \quad t_{da} \geq 0 \qquad (7.1)$$

The notation for the study of metrics used for the performance evaluation is shown in Table 7.1. A frame time that consists of three times, synchronization time, direct access time, and adaptive contention-free access time. The subsequent equation expresses a total frame period

Table 7.1 Meanings of notations used

Symbols	Definition
t_{fr}	Frame length time
t_{st}	Synchronization time
t_{da}	Direct access time
t_{ac}	Adaptive contention-free access time
N	Number of time slots
T_{ts}	Time of adaptive contention-free access slot
T_d	Data transmission period
T_{ack}	ACK packet period
T_{sifs}	Time of short interframe space
T_g	Time of guard
L_p	Data length
T_b	Time of transmission or receiving a byte
T_{cw}	Contention window time
T_{ifs}	Time of inter frame space
$E[t]$	Expected time of a reservation procedure
H_{max}	Maximum number of hops
d_{rate}	Data generated rate
N_{hops}	Number of hops
τ	Transmission probability for a node in any time slot
$P^{H_{max}-1}$	Probability of maximum hops

$$t_{fr} = t_{st} + t_{da} + t_{ac} \tag{7.2}$$

The adaptive contention-free access phase is separated into N time periods. Therefore, adaptive contention-free access period is represented as the product of N and time period as

$$t_{ac} = N * T_{ts} \tag{7.3}$$

A time period should have sufficient time to send and receive data packets. As shown in Eq. 7.4, T_{ts} is the overall time consumed for data transmission time, ACK packet time, receiving time which is three times of short interframe space time and time of guard. The overall time consumed is calculated as

$$T_{ts} = T_d + T_{ack} + 3 * T_{sifs} + T_g \tag{7.4}$$

where $T_d = L_p / T_b$.

In further, the CSMA/CA method is allowed for channel acquisition. The random back-off system for contention follows IFS period. The typical value of the random back-off system is half of the contention gap size. The estimated time $E[t]$ of a reservation method is

$$E[t] = T_{ifs} + T_{cw}/2 + 2 * T_{sifs} \tag{7.5}$$

Reservation methods are performed in direct access time. So, the maximum number of completed reservation method H_{max} is the significance of direct access time divided by expected time of a reservation method.

$$H_{max} = [t_{da}/E[t]] \tag{7.6}$$

The probability of one extra hop's transmission within a frame time is required when the forwarding node reserves a prior time period than a time period of the relay node during the adaptive contention-free access phase. The probability P is represented in Eq. 7.7. It is assumed that the number of the unconditional time periods is m. If the forwarding node chooses a time period, the relay node chooses one of the following time periods other than the preferred time period. The probability is independent of the value m.

$$P = [1 - (1 - \tau)]^{(m-1)} \tag{7.7}$$

The probability of one more hop transmission to get the average hop count of the relayed packets in a frame time is expressed in Eq. 7.8. The probability of one more hop transmission is same regardless of the value of m, the average hop count of the relayed packets during a frame time is expressed as the sum of probability from one hop transmission to maximum hops transmission during a frame time.

$$E[MAX_h] = \sum H_{max} * P_{H_{max}-1} \tag{7.8}$$

The average end-to-end latency during the multi-hop transmission condition is obtained by first finding the average number of a frame time spent for multi-hop transmission. The significance is that the hop number from a source node to a sink node is divided by the average hop count of the relayed packets. The average end-to-end latency is equal to the product of the average number of a frame time. The Eq. 7.9 computes the average end-to-end latency as

$$[End\_to\_End]_{latency} = [N_{hop}/E[MAX_h] * t_{fr} \tag{7.9}$$

We assume that both arrival and service rate are constant and concern D/D/1 queuing representation in sensor nodes, where D/D/1 queuing delay is considered to be negligible. The arrival rate is smaller than the service rate. Conversely, there is a waiting delay due to channel contention. The constraint function of direct access time is the product of estimated time of a reservation method and data generated during a frame time.

$$t_{da} \geq E[t] * (d_{rate} * t_{fr}) \tag{7.10}$$

The following constraint is lowest number of time periods, i.e., the data generated in a frame time. The value N is numeral,

$$N \geq [d_{rate} * t_{fr} + 1] \tag{7.11}$$

The following equation gives the minimization for latency:
minimize $[End\_to\_End]_{latency}$ such   that $t_{da} \geq E[t] * (d_{rate} * t_{fr})$

$$N \geq [d_{rate} * t_{fr} + 1] \tag{7.12}$$

$$t_{da} \geq 0, and N \geq 0, \tag{7.13}$$

The optimal direct access time and number of time periods in each sensor node is calculated as per the data rate from the source node. Hence, the Eq. 7.14 depicts the final minimization expression of the end-to-end latency.

$$minimize[End\_to\_End]_{latency} = [N_{hop}/E[MAX_h] + 1] * (t_{st} + t_{da} + N * T_{ts})$$
$$\in t_{da} \geq 0 \, and \, N \geq 0$$
$$\tag{7.14}$$

7.5　Performance Evaluation

7.5.1　Simulation Setup

The performance of CBH-MAC has been evaluated using ns-2 simulator and compared with H-MAC and S-MAC. The topology is a ten-hop chain and cross network with source at the first node and sink at the end node as shown in Figs. 7.2 and 7.3. Two-ray ground indication model for radio transmission and omnidirectional antenna is used in this simulation. Each node is situated at a distance 200 m from the adjacent node and the carrier sensing range is 550 m. The following performance metrics are considered to evaluate the QoS in CBH-MAC networks. The simulation parameters of CBH-MAC are shown in Table 7.2.

1. Average End-to-End delay: It is expressed as the time taken for a packet to pass through from the CBR source node to the sink.

2. Packet delivery ratio (PDR): It is defined as the ratio of the number of data packets that are forwarded by the source to the number of data packets that are accepted by the sink.

3. Energy Consumption: The ratio of total consumption of energy during the simulation to the total number of sensor nodes in the wireless network. Two types of scenarios are used in the simulations: (i) Multi-hop Chain Topology and (ii) Multi-hop Cross Topology.

7.5.2　Multi-hop Chain Topology

Figure 7.2 shows chain topology, which consists of a single source node 1, a single sink node 11, with intermediate nodes addressing packets and relaying them in the direction of sink node 11. Every node is uniformly spaced at 200 m apart in a straight line. A single Constant Bit Rate (CBR) flow sends packets from the source node 1 to the sink node 11. The span of the chain varies from 1 to 14 hops.

Table 7.2 Simulation parameters

Parameters values	Receiving power
0.5 W	Transmission power
0.5 W	Idle power
0.05 W	Sleeping power
0.001 W	Simulation run time
1000 s	Channel coding
Manchester	S-MAC
10%	Duty cycle

7.5.3 Multi-hop Cross Topology

Figure 7.3 shows cross topology. The chains of nodes are placed at 200 m apart cross each other at the center node. Both the chains are of the same span and a single sensor node at the crossing position is allocated by the two chains. The two CBR flows exist, one along each chain of sensor nodes.

7.5.4 End-to-End Latency

End-to-End latency plays a very significant role in WSNs. It mentions the total time in use for a single packet to transmit across a network from the source node 1 to the sink node 11. There are many factors affecting the end-to-end latency, among them the routing path and the interference level. Figure 7.4 shows performance of end-to-end latency by means of varying number of hops. For the multi-hop chain topology, end-to-end latency in H-MAC, S-MAC, and CBH-MAC increases with the increase in hop length.

However, the end-to-end latency in Sensor Medium Access Control protocol increases at a much faster rate, because it has a lower duty cycle. CBH-MAC outperforms both H-MAC and S-MAC. In addition, our proposed CBH-MAC protocol makes lower end-to-end latency due to small collision rate of the reservation control packets. It stabilizes the sensor data traffic transmission throughout reservation of time period in adaptive contention-free access time.

Figure 7.5 depicts the end-to-end latency results of H-MAC, S-MAC, and CBH-MAC in multi-hop cross topology. Traffic contention is lower for CBH-MAC compared to H-MAC and S-MAC. CBH-MAC transmits packets quickly through the contention period, thus avoiding collisions. As shown in Fig. 7.3, the two sources generate CBR traffic simultaneously and flow through the intersection of the two chain topology without collision. Thus, both the data packets are delivered to their sink nodes, respectively.

We present our simulation results, End-to-End latency and compare them with the analytical results of the mathematical model. We have designed chain and cross topology by setting different hops, packet size, and packet arrival interval to evaluate the performance of CBH-MAC networks. For analysis purpose, we use only cross topology scenario, which consists of two sources that simultaneously generate their Constant Bit Rate traffic to intentionally create channel congestion at the intersection of two chains. From the results observed in Fig. 7.6, our analysis results agrees with the simulation quite well due to two reasons: 1. Each CBH-MAC node operates the reservation procedure and 2. Reserves time slot in adaptive contention-free successively in multi-hop.

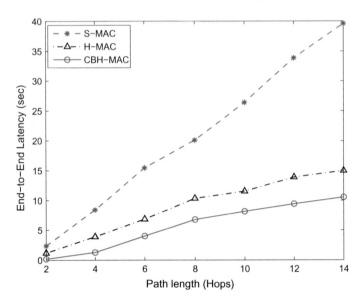

Fig. 7.4 End-to-end latency (s) in a 10-hop chain topology

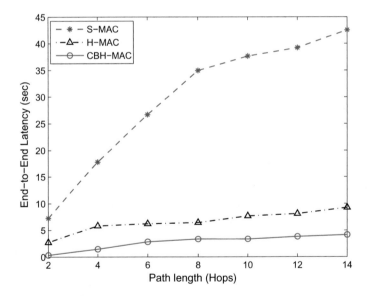

Fig. 7.5 End-to-end latency (s) in a 10-hop cross topology

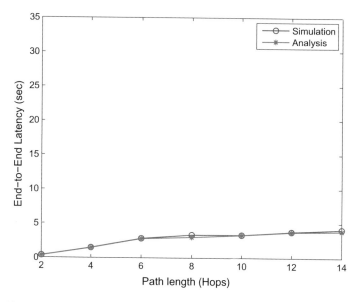

Fig. 7.6 Simulation versus analytical results in a 10-hop cross topology

7.5.5 Packet Delivery Ratio (PDR) Performance

Figures 7.7 and 7.8 show the performance of the packet delivery ratio under different packet arrival intervals (s) in chain and cross topologies. CBH-MAC performs better than S-MAC and H-MAC protocols. The packet arrival intervals are varied from 1 packet per second to 1 packet per 40 s to evaluate the network performance of CBH-MAC, H-MAC, and S-MAC. Figures 7.6 and 7.7 show our simulation results, CBH-MAC outperforms H-MAC and S-MAC by 11.11%.

7.5.6 Energy Consumption

The traffic load is varied with the packet arrival interval time. Multiple packets are sent in the cross and chain topology; every constant bit rate flow generates traffic load at the speed of 1 packet for every 5 s. H-MAC and S-MAC consume higher energy with the increase in packet arrival interval time, but CBH-MAC has a lower rate of increase than the other two protocols. It is observed in Figs. 7.9 and 7.10 that S-MAC node consumes less energy at packet arrival interval of time 5 s, than at packet arrival time of 10 s. This is in account of more packets being dropped at nodes due to collision at increased traffic loads, as the Medium Access Control layer does not cache more than one packet. CBH-MAC is more energy efficient than H-MAC and S-MAC. Both S-MAC and H-MAC consumes higher energy in cross topology than in chain topology, because of the difference in contention handling procedures by the two schemes.

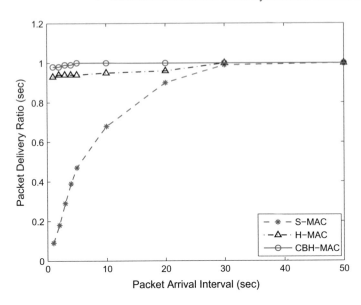

Fig. 7.7 Packet delivery ratio in a 10-hop chain topology

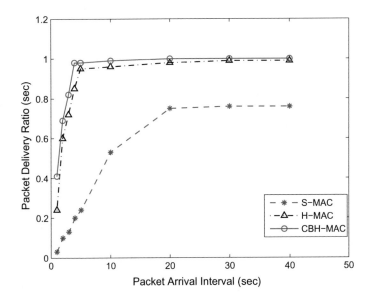

Fig. 7.8 Packet delivery ratio in a 10-hop cross topology

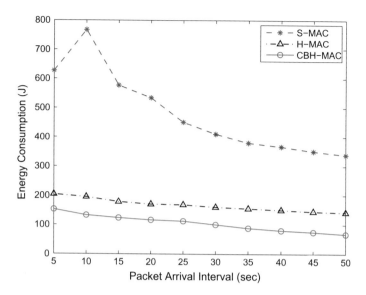

Fig. 7.9 Energy consumption in a 10-hop chain topology

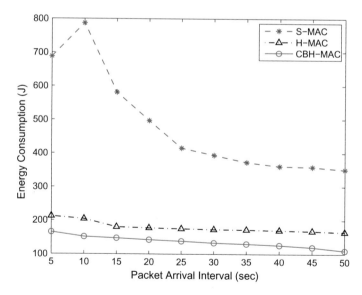

Fig. 7.10 Energy consumption in a 10-hop cross topology

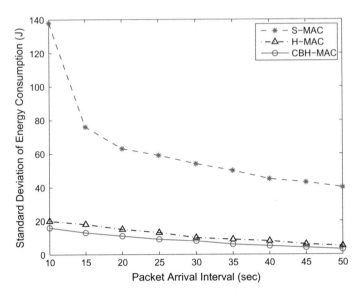

Fig. 7.11 Standard deviation of energy consumption in a 10-hop cross topology

As shown in Fig. 7.11, it is observed that the nodes remaining energy in CBH-MAC are more evenly distributed than in both Sensor-MAC and H-MAC. Therefore, CBH-MAC is efficient in contention handling, due to the reservation of time slots in adaptive contention-free access time and hence, increases the network lifetime.

7.6 Summary

This chapter presents CBH-MAC for cross and chain topology, a hybrid MAC protocol specifically considered for WSNs. It reduces the end-to-end latency for delay sensitive data traffic in multi-hop routing. In this case, a node operates the reservation method during contention-based phase and reserves a time period in the adaptive contention-free time. The neighboring nodes of the sender and receiver accept their individual reservation control packets. The reservation packets take place in nodes along the routing path. As a result, nodes reserve the time period successively in multi-hop. The simulation results demonstrate that the CBH-MAC protocol has significantly reduced end-to-end latency and improves energy efficiency and packet delivery ratio. It outperforms H-MAC and S-MAC in end-to-end latency, consumption of energy, and packet delivery ratio.

References

1. T.V. Dam, K. Langendoen, An adaptive energy-efficient MAC protocol for wireless sensor networks, in *1st ACM Conference on Embedded Networked SenSys* (2003), pp. 171–180
2. J. Polastre, J. Hill, D. Culler, Versatile low power media access for wireless sensor networks, in *2nd ACM Conference on Embedded Networked SenSys* (2004), pp. 95–107
3. G. Lu, B. Krishnamachari, C.S. Raghavendra, An adaptive energy-efficient and low-latency MAC for data gathering in wireless sensor networks, in *IEEE IPDPS* (2004), pp. 902–921
4. Y. John Heidenmann, D. Estrin, Access control with coordinated adaptive sleeping for wireless sensor networks, in *IEEE/ACM Transactions Networking*, vol. 12 (2004), pp. 493–506
5. Z. Chen, A. Khokhar, Self organization and energy efficient TDMA MAC protocol by wake up for wireless sensor networks, in *IEEE SECON* (2004), pp. 335–341
6. I. Rhee, A. Warrier, M. Aia, J. Min, MAC: a Hybrid MAC for wireless sensor networks, in *3rd ACM Conference on Embedded Networked SenSys* (2005), pp. 511–524
7. V. Rajendran, K. Obraczka, J. Garcia-Luna-Aceves, Energy-efficient collision free medium access control for wireless sensor networks, in *1st International Conference on Embedded Networked SenSys* (2003), pp. 181–192
8. I. Chlamtac, A. Farago, A.D. Myers, V.R. Syrotiuk, G.V. Zaruba, ADAPT: a dynamically self adjusting media access control protocol for AdHoc networks, *IEEE Globecom'99* (1999), pp. 11–15
9. A. Sridharan, B. Krishnamachari, Max-min fair collision-free scheduling for wireless sensor networks, in *IEEE International Conference* (2004), pp. 585–590
10. R. Mangharam, A. Rowe, R. Rajkumar, FireFly: a cross-layer platform for real-time sensor networks. Real-Time Syst. **37**, 183–231 (2007)
11. J. Chen, P. Zhu, P. Qi, PR-MAC: path-oriented real-time MAC protocol for wireless sensor networks, in *ICESS* (2007), pp. 530–539
12. T. Watteyne, I. Auge Blum, S. Ubeda, Dual-mode real-time MAC protocol for wireless sensor networks, in *IEEE* (2006)
13. Y. Kim, H. Shin, H. Cha, *Y-MAC: an energy-efficient multi-channel MAC protocol for dense wireless sensor networks, IPSN, St. Louis, Missouri, USA* (IEEE, 2008), pp. 53–63
14. O. Incel, S. Dulman, P. Jansen, Multi-channel support for dense wireless sensor networking, in *EuroSSC* (Springer, Netherlands, 2006), pp. 1–14
15. S. Du, A.K. Saha, D.B. Johnson, RMAC: a routing-enhanced duty-cycle MAC protocol for wireless sensor networks, in *INFOCOM* (Springer, Netherlands, 2007), pp. 1478–1486
16. H. Wang, X. Zhang, A. Khokhar, Cross-layer optimized medium access control to support Multihop QoS routing for WSNs. IEEE Trans. Vehicul. Technol., Hong Kong SAR, China **59**(5), 26–30 (2008)

Chapter 8
QMSR: Qos Multi-hop Sensor Routing Cross-Layer Design for WSNs

Abstract We have proposed a QoS Multi-hop Sensor Routing (QMSR) protocol that is developed for Mobile Wireless Sensor Networks (MWSNs). This protocol manages Admission Control Scheme (ACS) with minimum overhead resources for fresh flows without degrading the performance of the existing flows. ACS is an important strategy for regulating the parallel flows in a contention-based channels to meet the requirements of QoS. QMSR estimates the available bandwidth before allocating the resources on a per hop basis. The protocol minimizes the overall energy consumption and guarantees the end-to-end delay.

8.1 Introduction

In MWSNs, all sensor nodes are highly mobile in which they are distributed to transmit data packets. In a rapidly changing topology, every mobile node participates as a router in the detection and protection of paths to all the other nodes. The most important benefit of Mobile Wireless Sensor Networks are simple and fast deployment without fixed network.

The large numbers of mobile nodes have several access controls, to facilitate routing. The IEEE 802.11 Medium Access Control protocol in multi-hop Mobile Wireless Sensor Networks has been commonly used for different wireless networks and known for low collisions.

In MWSNs, nodes are mobile and they listen to their surrounding broadcasts to determine the paths to arrive at every other node. Scalability and Mobility are major issues in mobile wireless networks thus, it is necessary for efficient routing to exchange messages among the sensor nodes in multi-hop.

8.2 Related Works

Quality of Service (QoS) provisioning is one of the most important features of the WSNs. Call Admission System (CAS) is critical in maintaining satisfactory QoS to the admitted users. For each path request, CAS makes the decision of whether or not

© Springer Nature Singapore Pte Ltd. 2020
K. R. Venugopal et al., *QoS Routing Algorithms for Wireless Sensor Networks*,
https://doi.org/10.1007/978-981-15-2720-3_8

to accept the user. The decision is based on the number of resources allocated to the sink. The objective is to simultaneously guarantee QoS and achieve high resource utilization.

Wu et al. [1] develop a link-layer channel model that guarantees QoS parameters delay bounds, accuracy, efficiency in admission control and resource reservation. Karp et al. [2] propose a GPSR (Greedy Perimeter Stateless Routing) protocol that adapts a perimeter forwarding strategy to route messages. Abdrabou et al. [3] propose a MMPP (Markov Modulated Poisson Process) link-layer distributed model, a Call Admission Control (CAC) algorithm that provides stochastic delay guarantees.

Sarr et al. [4] adopts QoS-AODV passive approach, by defining a metric called Bandwidth Efficiency Ratio (BWER). Hello messages are employed which are periodically broadcast in the one-hop vicinity and efficiently utilize the bandwidth. Jain et al. [5] propose multiple orthogonal channels enhance throughput. Garces et al. [6] present mobile nodes that utilize only one channel at any instant, but the transceiver is still capable of switching from one channel to another.

Chakeres et al. [7] address the dynamically adapting PAC (Perceptive Admission Control) monitoring channel busy time that enables high network utilization. Akyildiz et al. [8] present a cross-layer module that incorporates initiative determination, receiver-based contention, distributed duty cycle operation, local congestion, residual energy to determine the rate of packets in progress.

Azad et al. [9] develop multiple sink placement strategy along the edges of sensor networks to increase the throughput and network lifetime. Jovanovic et al. [10] develop TFMAC protocol that chooses different frequencies in different slots to route packets to its neighbors. Javed et al. [11] design the OLSR (Optimized Link State Routing) protocol for mobile wireless networks. It provides the best routes with respect to the number of hops.

Bernardo et al. [12] propose the MMH-MAC (Mobile Multimode Hybrid-Medium Access Control) protocol for MWSNs. It employs synchronous mode for high throughput and asynchronous mode for energy efficiency. Nabi et al. [13] design a MCMAC (Mobile Cluster MAC), that reduces latency and energy consumption. Bhuiyan et al. [14] propose a Analytical study of IEEE 802.11 DCF protocols ensuring low latency, high delivery probability, and lower energy consumption.

Ngo et al. [15] propose a hybrid Versatile Medium Access Control (VMAC) that employs contention-free MAC protocol for energy saving and contention-based protocol for short transmissions. Khalek et al. [16] develop a optimized flow with minimum consumption of energy and low end-to-end delay for video distribution wireless networks. Haitao et al. [17] present IEEE 802.11 wireless multi-hop protocol by considering channel capacity to allocate network resource for data packet forwarding.

Javaid et al. [18] discuss Square Routing Protocol with Mobile Sink (SRP-MS) that use effective weight balancing among mobile nodes resulting in good throughput and enhanced network lifetime. Gonga et al. [19] present MobiSense protocol which is a cross-layer design for low mobility nodes with reduced latency and energy-efficient communication. Abdrabou et al. [20] discuss a QoS routing scheme for IEEE 802.11 Ad hoc networks that guarantees specified delays for bursty traffic. It chooses routes based on an environmental on demand ad hoc routing scheme.

8.3   System Model and Problem Definition

We design MWSNs, in which each mobile sensor node can travel all over the network as shown in Fig. 8.1. Admission Control Scheme is necessary to control the number of concurrent streams and to meet the desired Quality of Service. The mobile sensor node collects data from their environment/atmosphere through multi-hops and transmits to the sink. The main objectives of the work are to

  (i) Provide resource in end-to-end basis.
 (ii) Ensure quick and consistent routing scheme.
(iii) Ensure end-to-end QoS for real-time application.

  The assumptions are

  (i) Every mobile sensor node has identical capacity for computation, sensing, and mobility.
 (ii) The initial mobile node position is random.
(iii) All nodes have complete information about their adjacent nodes.

  QMSR cross-layer routing scheme is a low-powered, wide communication channel and has faultless synchronization among every mobile node. Mobile Wireless

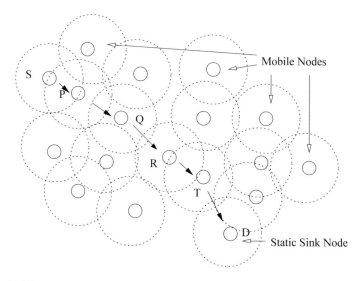

Fig. 8.1 Mobile network topology for path detection with static sink node

Sensor Networks use scattered, random access control protocol which needs perfect estimation of packet transmission period for efficient delivery. The back-off instance is slotted, which depends on the physical layer standard. Many mobile nodes are allowed to transmit at the commencement of every slot period. The wireless medium is shared and actively allocated to the mobile nodes.

The proposed scheme uses the Admission Control Scheme (ACS) and Resource Reservation (RR) procedure which is strongly depend on IEEE 802.11 DCF MAC layer. Every mobile node access the medium randomly for data transmission through a four-way RTS/CTS/DATA/ACK handshake signal. The QMSR is a cross-layer routing scheme that achieves path detection, path preservation, and ACS for MWSNs without affecting the QoS of the existing admitted streams. This routing scheme determines the path detection and multiple path preservation that offers the necessary QoS involving the source node and the sink sensor node.

In the path detection procedure, the mobile node attempts to forward packets to a sink node. Initially, it checks the route cache to find out if there are bandwidth availability and path to the sink node. The mobile nodes keep track of hello packets. After that, the mobile sensor node transmits a path-demand ($pdem$) packet to the neighbor nodes. The path locating mechanism utilizes reactive on demand path messages in the entire WSNs to obtain a path from the mobile source node to the sink node. These messages are exchanged between the mobile nodes periodically.

The aim of the path preservation process is significant, particularly in the case of a mobile node. The mobile node accepts an invalid path fault ($pfault$) packet, when there is a wireless link fault on the path, if a mobile node does not accept a hello packet from a neighbor node. The path is removed in the cache of the path. For path preservation, a fresh $pdem$ packet is generated.

8.4   QMSR Algorithm

The proposed QMSR algorithm assures successful resource allocation and prevents collisions and ensures end-to-end Quality of Service for real-time applications. Let dtn, denote the distance between two sensor nodes (X_i, Y_j) such nodes belong to L. The algorithm focuses on low-energy, fault-free communication medium, and faultless synchronization between every mobile sensor node. QMSR protocol is as shown in Algorithm 8.1.

8.5   Performance Evaluation

The evaluation of QMSR by using the ns-2 simulator having 60 mobile nodes and these nodes move as per random waypoint system. Mobile node moves randomly with a velocity of 1 m/s in the region of 700 m $\times$ 700 m. The exponential traffic streams produced on/off at the mobile nodes with 5 s as typical off time and 0.4 s as

---

Algorithm 8.1: Qos Multi-hop Sensor Routing Cross-Layer Design (QMSR)

---

1 Initialize hop_count = 0;
2 **for** $i = 1$ *to Sink_node* **do**
3 | **if** *Sink_node is in table* **then**
4 | | **if** *availBW > reqBW* **then**
5 | | | Broadcast pdem;
6 | | | Check the path table to find next node exists;
7 | | | If so, send hello packet;
8 | | | availBW = resource_allocate;
9 | | | Calculate distance between nodes;
10 | | | dtn = d(Xi, Yj) ∈ i , j ∈ L, i ≠ j;
11 | | | hop_count = hop_count + 1;
12 | | **else**
13 | | | discard pdem;
14 | **else**
15 | | pfault packet;

---

typical on time. Simulation is carried out with the highest node velocity varying in the range 5–15 m/s with a pause period zero. The data rates of every transfer stream have a peak speed of 600 Kilo bits per second with a delay bound of 100 ms. The existing traffic stream is increased from 9 to 18 streams. The parameters useful for evaluating the performance of the QMSR are given below.

Packet Delivery: It can be expressed as the ratio of data packets sent to the sink, produced by the source nodes. Figure 8.2 depicts that the packet delivery percentage of traffic streams of the proposed QMSR scheme is from 97 to 100% for different velocity of mobile nodes. The high percentage of this protocol indicates that the majority of the packets are being delivered toward the upper layers.

Percentage Drop Rate: The ratio of the number of streams of reduced data packets to the number of the admitted streams because of the ACS. Figure 8.3 depicts the data drop rate by varying mobile node velocity, i.e., 5, 10, and 15 m/s. The number of packets dropped increases with the velocity of the mobile node and finally, the drop rate decreases to below 3% of the self-governing node density of the network and low mobility of the nodes.

Percentage Overhead: It is the ratio of the number of control bytes generated by the routing scheme to the number of data bytes expected at the destination. The overhead percentage is a significant parameter for computing the scalability of a QMSR for cross-layer scheme. Figure 8.4, depicts the routing overhead of QMSR for varying node mobility, i.e., 5, 10, and 15 m/s. As the mobility of node is increased, the *pdem* packets fail to reach the sink. Then, extra *pdem* packets are retransmitted and there is a possibility of collisions because of control packets and hence increased overhead.

Admission Ratio Percentage: It is described as the number of data traffic streams admitted from the source nodes to the wireless network. The admission ratio of QMSR scheme reduces with the increase in the number of simultaneous traffic

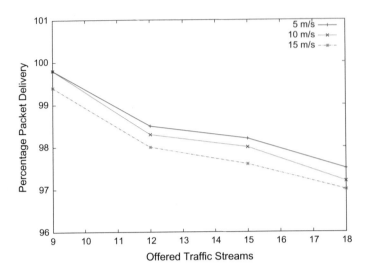

Fig. 8.2 Percentage packet delivery of QMSR by sensor node mobility

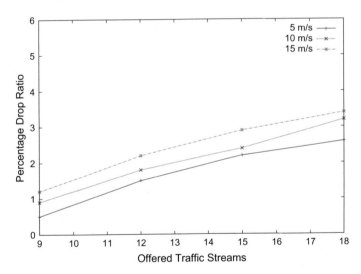

Fig. 8.3 Drop ratio percentage of QMSR with different number of mobility

streams as shown in Fig. 8.5 and is affected by the velocity of mobile nodes, i.e., higher the mobility of nodes, lower is the admission ratio.

Energy Consumption: The scheme QMSR uses a lower amount of energy consumption for velocities ranging from 1 to 15 m/s, since it needs the least number of routing messages. At lower velocity, the topology changes are less frequent and thus consumption of energy is low. Conversely, as velocity goes up, extra route modification is required; producing more routing packets and consumption of energy is high.

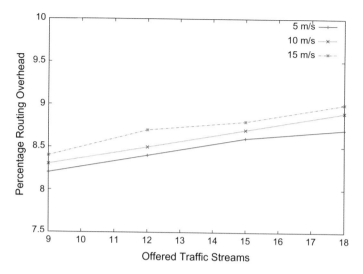

Fig. 8.4 Routing overhead of QMSR with different node mobility

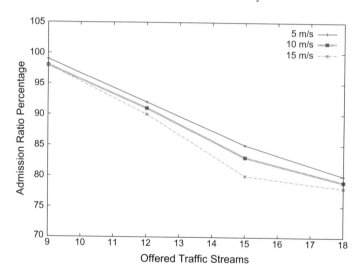

Fig. 8.5 Admission ratio percentage of QMSR with various sensor node mobility

QMSR consumes the least energy compared to DSR and DSDV schemes as shown in Fig. 8.6.

The QMSR discovers multi-hop route establishment using Admission Control Scheme. As shown in the Fig. 8.7, the number of admitted streams reduces with the rise in a peak data rate. The Admission Control Scheme achieves increased network utilization, with the increase in the number of admitted streams. The amount of admitted streams in QMSR (Simulation) is almost similar to the QMSR (Theoretical).

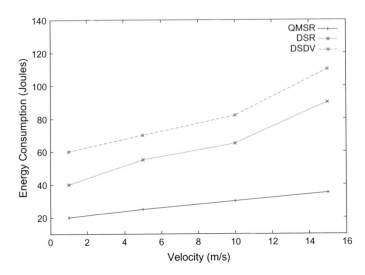

Fig. 8.6 Consumption of energy for various routing protocols with mobility model

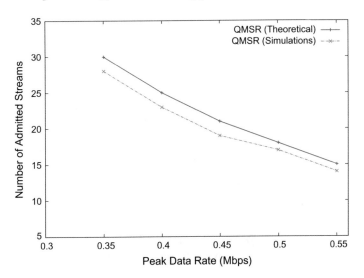

Fig. 8.7 Admitted streams from proposed QMSR with various peak data rates

The performance of QMSR does not weaken even after the rise in the number of offered streams. The QMSR is quicker in determining the new paths to the static sink node and gives improved performance than DSDV [21] and DSR [22].

8.6 Summary

Mobility is a significant feature in the design of a routing scheme for MWSNs. The QMSR makes a choice for admitting resource share with low message overhead and estimates the offered bandwidth at the Medium Access Control layer. Path detection is mainly focused on link strength and packet delivery. The QMSR scheme manages ACS for fresh streams without affecting the Quality of Service of existing streams with negligible overhead. Result shows that the Admission Control Scheme can successfully control the traffic streams with enhanced bandwidth utilization. QMSR results in reduced total consumption of energy and guarantees end-to-end delay on all network paths.

References

1. D. Wu, R. Negi, Effective capacity-based quality of service measures for wireless networks. ACM Mob. Netw. Appl. **11**(1), 9199 (2006)
2. B. Karp, H.T. Kung, Greedy perimeter stateless routing for WSNs, in *Proceedings of ACM/IEEE International Conference on MCN* (2000), pp. 243–254
3. A. Abdrabou, W. Zhuang, Stochastic delay guarantees and statistical call admission control for IEEE 802.11 single-hop Adhoc networks. IEEE Trans. Wirel. Commun. **7**(10), 3972–3981 (2008)
4. C. Sarr, C. Chaudet, G. Chelius, I.G. Lassou, Improving accuracy in available bandwidth estimation for 802.11-based Ad Hoc networks, in *Proceedings of IEEE International Conference on Mobile Adhoc and Sensor Systems (MASS)* (2006), pp. 517–520
5. N. Jain, S. Das, A. Nasipuri, A multi-channel CSMA MAC protocol with multiple receiver-based channel selection for multi-hop wireless networks, in *Proceedings of IEEE Tenth International Conference on Computer Communications and Networks (ICCCN)* (2001), pp. 432–439
6. R. Garces, J.J. Garcia Luna Aceves, Collision avoidance and resolution multiple access for multichannel wireless networks, in *Proceedings of IEEE INFOCOM*, vol. 2 (2000), pp. 595–602
7. I.D. Chakeres, E.M. Belding Royer, PAC: perceptive admission control for mobile wireless networks, in *Proceedings of IEEE International Conference on Quality of Service in Heterogeneous Wired/Wireless Networks (QSHINE)* (2004), pp. 18–26
8. I.F. Akyildiz, M.C. Vuran, O.B. Akan, A cross-layer protocol for wireless sensor networks, in *Proceedings of Conference on Information Science and Systems (CISS)* (2006), pp. 22–24
9. A.P. Azad, A. Chockalingam, Mobile base stations placement and energy aware routing in WSNs (2006)
10. M. Jovanovic, G. Djordjevic, TFMAC: multi-channel MAC protocol for wireless sensor networks, in *Proceedings of 8th International Conference on Telecommunications in Modern Satellite, Cable and Broadcasting Services (TELSIKS)* (2007)
11. S. Javed, A. Furqan-ul-Islam, A. Pirzada, Performance analysis of OLSR protocol in A MAWN, in *Proceedings of IEEE (IC4)* (2009), pp. 17–18
12. L. Bernardo, H. Agua, M. Pereira, R. Oliveira, A MAC protocol for MWSNs with Bursty traffic, in *Proceedings of WCNC* (2010), pp. 1–6
13. M. Nabi, M. Blagojevic, M. Geilen, T. Basten, MCMAC: an optimized medium access control protocol for mobile clusters in wireless sensor networks, in *Proceedings of IEEE Sensor Mesh and Ad Hoc Communications and Networks (SECON)* (2010), pp. 1–9

14. Bhuiyan, M. Masumuzzaman, Cross layer modelling of contention-based MAC and deterministic routing protocols in multi-hop WSNs, in *Proceedings of IEEE International Conference on Information Networking (ICOIN)* (2011), pp. 74–79
15. V. Ngo, A. Anpalagan, I. Woungang, Versatile medium access control (VMAC) protocol for mobile sensor networks, in *Proceedings of 7th IEEE Wireless Communications and Mobile Computing Conference (IWCMC)* (2011), pp. 836–841
16. A.A. Khalek, Z. Dawy, Energy-efficient cooperative video distribution with statistical QoS provisions over wireless networks. IEEE Trans. Mob. Comput. **11**(7), 1223–1236 (2012)
17. Z. Haitao, D. Yuning, L. Nanjie, T. Feng, Z. Hui, Adaptive optimal capacity perception and control for wireless multi-hop networks. China Commun. **9**(11), 23–30 (2012)
18. N. Javaid, A.A. Khan, M. Akbar, Z.A. Khan, SRP-MS: a routing protocol for delay tolerant WSNs, in *Proceedings of 26th CCECE* (2013), pp. 1–4
19. A. Gonga, O. Landsiedel, M. Johansson, MobiSense: power efficient micro-mobility in wireless sensor networks, in *Proceedings of IEEE Distributed Computing in Sensor Systems and Workshops (DCOSS)* (2011), pp. 1–8
20. A. Abdrabou, W. Zhuang, Statistical QoS routing for IEEE 802.11 Multihop Ad Hoc networks. IEEE Trans. Wirel. Commun. **8**(3), 1542–1552 (2009)
21. C.E. Perkins, P. Bhagwat, *Highly Dynamic Destination-Sequenced Distance-Vector Routing (DSDV) for Mobile Computers, SIGCOMM* (ACM, London, 1994)
22. D.B. Johnson, Routing in Ad Hoc networks of mobile hosts, in *Proceedings of the Workshop on Mobile Computing Systems and Applications* (IEEE Computer Society, Santa Cruz, CA, 1994), pp. 158–163

Chapter 9
EPC: Efficient Gateway Selection for Passive Clustering in MWSNs

Abstract Passive clustering does not employ control packets to collect topological information in a Mobile Wireless Sensor Networks (MWSNs). The primary objective is to make Passive Clustering more practical, robust, and to minimize the quantity of cluster information on the data packets. In this chapter, we propose an intelligent gateway selection heuristic along with a time-out mechanism and an efficient passive clustering algorithm that employs an optimal number of gateways to reduce the number of rebroadcast and improve the QoS of the network. In this proposal, we avoid making frequent changes in cluster architecture, caused due to repeated election and re-election of cluster heads and gateways.

9.1 An Introduction to Clustering

Clustering is based on partitioning of a network into logical substructures called *clusters*. A cluster is a set of nodes which can be treated as a single entity during packet transmission. Each node in a cluster assumes a role depending on its position in the cluster and other topological information. The most important role in a cluster is played by the *Clusterhead*. A cluster cannot exist without a cluster head, as it is the only node which interacts with other clusters. In the clustering scheme, a node can send packets to other nodes of the same cluster, without the help of a cluster head. A node that belongs to more than one cluster becomes a *Gateway*. A gateway is responsible for routing packets across two clusters as they are reachable from both the clusters in a single hop. The remaining nodes are known as *Ordinarynodes*, and they do not have the privilege of routing packets to nodes of the other cluster. The cluster architecture is shown in Fig. 9.1.

The stability of the cluster architecture is primarily determined by the rules used for selecting cluster heads and gateways. These rules must be so designed, as to make minimal architectural changes in the network whenever its topology changes. The

Reprinted by permission from Springer Nature: Springer LNCS-3741, T. Shiva Prakash, C. Aravinda, A. P. Deepak, S. Kamal, H. L. Mahantesh, K. R. Venugopal, L. M. Patnaik, Efficient Passive Clustering and Gateway Selection MANETs, IWDC'05, Copyright (2005).

© Springer Nature Singapore Pte Ltd. 2020
K. R. Venugopal et al., *QoS Routing Algorithms for Wireless Sensor Networks*,
https://doi.org/10.1007/978-981-15-2720-3_9

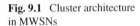

Fig. 9.1 Cluster architecture in MWSNs

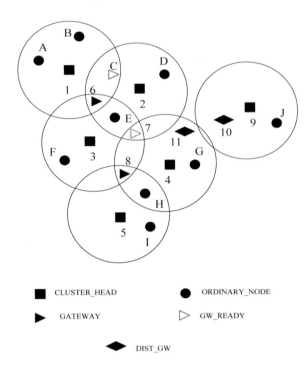

two most popular heuristics for cluster head or gateway selection are *Least Id* [1] and *First declaration wins rule* [2].

Routing protocols for WSNs can either be *flat or hierarchical*. Hierarchical routing protocols can reduce routing table storage and processing overhead, and therefore achieve better scalability. The most widely used two-level infrastructures are Dominant Set Pruning [3] and Clustering [1]. This work addresses the issue of scalability with respect to an increase in the number of control packets using passive clustering. This form of clustering is employed to reduce the number of rebroadcasts. Further, passive clustering works well only under ideal conditions. This can be justified by a number of peculiar cases of network topology, which are frequent in a WSN environment. These cases show that the control information piggy-backed on the data packets is alone not sufficient to maintain the cluster at all times. A survey [4] of different clustering algorithms for WSNs highlights their objectives, features, complexity, etc, and allso comparison of these clustering algorithms based on metrics such as convergence rate, cluster stability, cluster overlapping, location-awareness ,and support for node mobility.

9.2 Related Works

The problem of blind flooding is addressed in [5–8]. Several ideas have been proposed on reducing broadcast redundancy in wireless networks [9]. One of the most popular algorithm is *max-min d*-cluster formation [10]. This algorithm assumes that all links are bidirectional. It uses beacons to detect the presence of neighbors. If a node does not send beacons for a long time, it is assumed that it has either moved out or it has gone down. Though this algorithm works well, it should be triggered whenever the topology changes.

Bandwidth is a scarce resource in WSNs primarily because the nodes behave as routers in addition to being sources and destinations for the packets. Gupta and Kumar [11] proved that the performance of a wireless network decreases significantly with the increase in the number of nodes. This can be mainly attributed to the increase in the number of control packets with an increase in the number of nodes in the network. Also, movement of nodes causes failure of existing routes and fresh control packets will have to be used to detect new routes.

Grossglauser and Tse have proposed a mechanism to employ mobility of nodes to increase the capacity of WSNs using a different kind of packet-relaying approach. In this approach, a node hands-off packets to the destination only when it gets close to the packet's destination [12]. However, the packet-transit delay cannot be predicted as the nodes do not move in a predetermined way. Also, this approach cannot be used for real-time applications. Passive clustering uses ongoing data packets to extract information about the network. Thus, use of control packets is reduced. Passive clustering can be used to ensure scalability in a wireless network without resulting in a decline in its performance. Since bandwidth is limited in a wireless network, it is important to construct a virtual backbone consisting of only a subset of nodes that have the privilege to forward packets. Such a virtual backbone called *spine* plays an important role in routing, broadcasting, and connectivity management. An effort should be made to keep this backbone thin and connected [13–15].

Wan et al. [16] have described the formation of virtual backbone in ad hoc networks by means of a connected dominating set of nodes. In a connected dominating set (CDS), the number of nodes responsible for routing is reduced to the number of nodes in a CDS. Several heuristics have been put forth to find a minimum connected dominating set. Finding a minimum connected dominating set in a graph is NP-complete [17].

Clustering provides a mechanism to group the nodes. Clustering causes improvement in channel access, routing capabilities, code separation (among clusters), and bandwidth allocation [18, 19]. Clustering is classified into two types, active and passive. Some of the common algorithms employed in clustering are Least_ID, Highest_ID [20], Highest_connectivity [18], and LCC (Least cluster head change) [21].

The basic clustering algorithm was proposed by Lin and Gerla [1] based on the Least Id principle. It uses periodic control messages to maintain clusters and is known as active clustering. An innovative mechanism for cluster formation is provided in [2]. This method does not use any explicit control messages. Instead, it piggybacks the control information on the out-going data packets and has the advantage of reducing the control overhead. But, relying only on data packets for control information introduces a number of problems.

Williams et al. [22] classified the protocols as Simple Flooding, Probability-Based Methods, Area-Based Methods, and Neighbor knowledge methods based on algorithmic complexity and each node's state need. The existing reactive protocols like DSR [23], AODV [24] have high rebroadcast messages and control overhead.

Jin et al. [25] develop a clustering protocol in which passive clustering is implemented in the first round followed by active clustering in the next rounds, this helps to satisfy the requirements of energy efficiency and QoS in WMSNs. A smart delay approach helps to distribute the cluster uniformly along with cluster head based on a node disjoint many to one multipath routing discovery algorithm, which is comprised of an optimal path searching process and multipath expansion process.

Liu et al. [26] develop an innovative vehicular clustering design combining hierarchical clustering using classical routing algorithms. The results are compared with Direct, LEACH, and DCHS and the new protocol reduces hot stops in WSNs.

Chen et al. [27] propose a directional geographical routing (DGR) with forward error correction (FEC) coding aimed at real-time videos transmitted over energy and bandwidth limited unreliable WSNs. The protocol employs multiple disjointed paths for video sensor node using H.26L and helps in load balancing, bandwidth aggregation, and fast packet delivery.

Xiao et al. [28] investigate the fundamental performance limits of medium access control (MAC) protocols for particular multi-hop, RF-based wireless sensor networks, and underwater sensor networks. A key aspect of this study is the modeling of a fair-access criterion that requires sensors to have an equal rate of underwater frame delivery to the base station. Tight upper bounds on network utilization and tight lower bounds on the minimum time between samples are derived for fixed linear and grid topologies.

Xiao et al. [28] study the working boundaries of medium access control (MAC) protocols in RF underwater sensor nodes. Modeling of a fair access benchmark is conducted that considers that sensors have an equal rate of underwater frame delivery to the base station. Derivation of upper and lower limits of network utilization and minimum time between samples for fixed linear and grid topologies are conducted.

In [29], sensor nodes are segregated into important and non-critical nodes without any extra transmission. This Passive clustering uses 2-b piggybacking and monitoring user traffic making initial flooding efficient. Also, Passive clustering aids in density adaptation and minimizes control overhead of sensor routing protocols and improves scalability.

In [31], the proposed HMR-LEACH algorithm (Hierarchical Multipath Routing-LEACH) improves election of cluster head and adopts multi-hop algorithm instead of one hop transmission data. When chooses transmission path, HMR-LEACH algorithm takes energy and distance into account and assigns a probability to each transmitting path by weight. Simulation result indicates that HMR-LEACH outperforms the LEACH algorithm and prolongs the life of the network dramatically.

Wang et al. [30] propose trust-based clustering called LEACH-TM; here, trust is used to select the cluster heads and CHs are used as routers. Results indicate improvement in reliability of data transmission and lifetime of networks. Hierarchical Multipath Routing-LEACH (HMR-LEACH) is proposed in [31]; the protocol improves cluster head selection and uses multi-hop approach instead of one-hop transmission. HMR-LEACH algorithm considers energy and distance and assigns a probability to each transmitting path by weight. Simulation result proves that HMR-LEACH exceeds the LEACH algorithm and increases the life of the network.

A cluster-based QoS multipath routing protocol (CQMRP) is proposed by Lu et al. [32], the protocol provides QoS responsive routes in a scalable and flexible way in WSNs by maintaining local routing information of other clusters rather than a global state data. A cluster-based multipath delivery scheme (CMDS) is proposed by Jing et al. [33], which uses cluster and multipath to boost the capability of load balance, and prolong the network lifetime.

Bhatia et al. [34] present an improved version of AODV called Multipath Energy Aware AODV routing (ME-AODV), which utilizes the topology of network to divide it into one or more logical clusters and restricts the flooding of route request outside the cluster. The mesh links created at the time of cluster formation are used to decrease the routing path. ME-AODV uses nodes of the same cluster to share routing information, which significantly reduces the route path discovery. Since ZigBee routing is based on the shortest-hop count, which causes overuse of a small set of nodes and hence decreases node as well as network lifetime. They also propose a mix of Ad hoc On-demand Multipath Distance Vector routing (AOMDV) and Minimal-Battery Cost Routing (MBCR) as an extension to AODV to increase the lifetime of network. Bidai et al. [35] propose a multipath routing where multiple paths are used simultaneously to transfer data between a source and the sink. Also they propose Z-MHTR, a node disjoint multipath routing extension of the ZigBee hierarchical tree routing protocol in cluster-tree WSN.

A augmented version of AODV called Multipath Energy Aware AODV routing (ME-AODV) is proposed by Bhatia et al. [34]; here; the algorithm uses the topology of network to partition it into one or more logical clusters and diminish the flooding of route request outside the cluster. The mesh links built at cluster formation are used to reduce the routing path length. ME-AODV uses nodes of the same cluster to distribute routing information, this naturally reduces the route path exploration. The protocol uses Ad hoc On-demand Multipath Distance Vector routing (AOMDV) and Minimal-Battery Cost Routing (MBCR) as an expansion to AODV to boost the lifetime of network.

A Secure Cluster-based Multipath Routing protocol was proposed by Almalkawi et al. [36] for multimedia traffic that needs to deliver different data types of high data rate. The protocol uses the cluster heads and the optimized multiple paths to maintain timeliness and reliability of multimedia data communication with minimum energy requirements, additionally a secure key handling scheme prevents against attacks.

An innovative heuristics is proposed by Hafid et al. [37] which used passive clustering and achieves balanced energy consumption among the network nodes. The proposed scheme does not have stringent requirements such as clock synchronization and does not generate extra control traffic and can be seamlessly used with other clustering protocols.

Bandyopadhyay et al. [38] have used stochastic geometry with a distributed, randomized algorithm for generating clusters of sensors. This helps in reducing the total transmissions required to gather one sample from each sensor. The proposed protocol performs better with respect to energy costs than the max-min d-cluster algorithms.

9.3 Network Model

9.3.1 Definitions

- A Free Tree or an *Unrooted Tree* in a Mobile Wireless Sensor Network is defined as a connected graph with no cycles. A graph $G(V, E, n)$ is a free tree if G is connected, contains no cycles, and has n-1 edges.
- A Cluster is a group of nodes that is treated as a single entity, with reference to routing of packets.
- A Cluster Set is the set of all Cluster IDs to which a node belongs.
- A Cluster Head is a representative of the cluster, holding the privilege of forwarding packets to other members in that cluster.
- A Gateway is a node that connects overlapping clusters, capable of receiving/forwarding packets from/to the Cluster Heads of all the clusters to which it belongs.
- A Gateway Ready node (gw_ready) is a candidate gateway that has not yet detected enough gateways, it can become an ordinary node with the discovery of enough gateways.
- A Critical Path is a link between any two nodes or any two clusters, the loss of which results in loss of connectivity between the participating nodes or clusters.
- The Control Overhead is defined as the ratio of the number of control packets and the number of packets received by the destination node.
- The Competition Count (C_c) of a node is defined as the number of times a node competes for the Gateway status. It is set to zero, each time a node acquires either *initial or cluster head* status.
- The Redundancy Factor (R_f) of the network is defined as the maximum number of common clusters that any two neighboring gateways can connect. It has a minimum value of one and a maximum value of five, since a node cannot be a member of more than six clusters.

Fig. 9.2 Simple wireless network

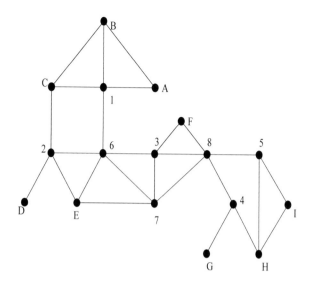

9.3.2 Mobile Wireless Sensor Network as a Graph

Let $G = (V, E)$ be a graph representing the topology of the network of mobile nodes, where E is a subset of $\{(v_i, v_j) \mid v_i, v_j \in V \wedge v_i \neq v_j\}$, set of finite links.

Figure 9.2, is an undirected graph representing a wireless network. A bidirectional link exists between two nodes if they are within the transmission range. Further, the network becomes a free tree [39] after passive clustering is applied to the network. This is the case when there are no redundant gateways. Only the nodes that lie in the path from source to destination in a free tree forward packets, while all the other nodes in the network are passive. In Fig. 9.3, the cluster heads are $(1, 2, 3, 4, 5)$ and the gateways are $(6, 8)$. Packets are routed through a series of ClusterHeads and Gateways between the source and destination.

9.4 Problem Definition

Given a wireless sensor network $G_w(V, E, n)$ of a finite set of nodes, $V = \{v_1, v_2, \ldots, v_n\}$ and a finite set of links $E = \{(v_i, v_j) \mid v_i, v_j \in V \wedge v_i \neq v_j\}$, a link is said to exist between two nodes v_i and v_j if they are within the transmission range of each other. The objectives are to

- account for mobility among nodes and to avoid loss of connectivity,
- reduce the number of rebroadcasts by reducing the number of redundant gateways between the overlapping clusters,

Fig. 9.3 Free tree

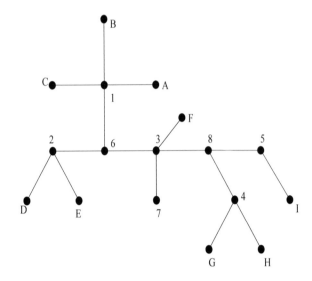

- ensure full coverage of all nodes within the given area using minimum number of clusters,
- reduce the quantity of control information loaded on the data packets,
- make the cluster architecture more stable,
- improve the QoS of the network.

   The assumptions are

- The network model assumes that the sensor nodes move in a two-dimensional area.
- The logical link layer is assumed to be free from errors.
- Each node is a unit disk. All nodes have equal transmission range.
- All transmitted packets are received in the order of their transmission.

9.4.1 Topological Problems Associated with Passive Clustering

Problem 1: An ordinary node may move into other clusters and generate a spurious gateway.

   In Fig. 9.4, w belongs to C_2 and has information about head of C_2. If it moves to C_1 as shown in Fig. 9.4, it starts receiving packets from the head of $C_1(Ch1)$, and updates its cluster table to have information about C_1 while retaining information about C_2. In this situation, it enters into gw_ready state and further, it may become a Gateway.

Fig. 9.4 Ordinary node
moving into other cluster

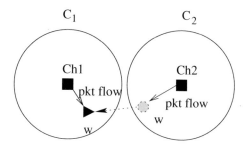

Fig. 9.5 Movement of
gateway

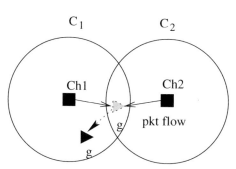

This is highly unacceptable, because (i) it may cause the real gateway candidate to become *ordinary*, resulting in the loss of connectivity between two clusters. (ii) it will have privilege to rebroadcast, which it should not have, resulting in an increase in the number of rebroadcasts and hence an increase in the traffic.

Problem 2: A gateway may move from the intersection area to a single cluster without relinquishing the status of the Gateway.

In Fig. 9.5, g is a gateway between $Ch1$ and $Ch2$ and it receives packets from both these cluster heads. Suppose g moves into C_1, now it belongs to only one cluster and hence must become an ordinary node. Instead, it continues to assume that it belongs to two clusters and hence will stay in gateway state, rebroadcasting the incoming packets. In passive clustering, a node gets good news (addition of new nodes or clusters) more easily than the bad news (a node going down or cluster head going out of the cluster).

Problem 3: Spurious generation of multiple gateways.

In a dense network, there will be a number of nodes in the intersection region of any two clusters. All of them compete for the *Gateway* status and the one with the *least id* wins. However, if the cluster sets of all the competing gateways are not exactly the same, then all of them become gateways. This creates redundant gateways and causes a broadcast storm in the wireless network.

Problem 4: Formation of redundant clusters.

During the initial setup, all the nodes that receive packets from the ordinary nodes become cluster heads. This results in dense and overlapped clusters.

Problem 5: Problems associated with the cluster head moving out of a cluster.

If an ordinary node does not receive packets from its cluster head for a long time, it assumes that cluster head is still present but it has no packets to send. An ordinary node has no privilege to rebroadcast, hence it relays on its cluster head to route packets to a distant node. Now, the ordinary node knows nothing about its cluster head's absence continues to send packets to the cluster head to route them to the destination resulting in the loss of packets and redundant broadcasts by the source. This problem can be solved only by electing a new cluster head among the other members of that cluster. This will not happen, because a node changes its state only on receiving packets from the other nodes. This is the case of a deadlock.

9.5   Algorithm EPC (Efficient Passive Clustering)

In the cluster architecture, a node can be in any of the following states: *initial, ordinary_node, gw_ready, gateway, dist_gw, cluster_head* as in Fig. 9.1. The algorithm is as follows:

(i) At the start, all the nodes are in the *initial* state and they are assigned a unique ID.

(ii) The source node sends a packet to all its neighbors and declares itself as a Cluster Head.

(iii) If the *initial* node hears from a *cluster_head*, it becomes an *ordinary_node*.

(iv) If a node (other than *initial* and *cluster_head*) hears from a non-Cluster Head,

    (a) It checks whether the sender node was a Cluster Head before. This check is carried out by scanning its cluster table in search of the sending node's ID. (Cluster Table maintains a list of Cluster Heads reachable from the node).

    (b) If the sender node was a Cluster Head before, then its entry is cleared from the cluster table of the receiving node. Packets from this node are not forwarded henceforth.

    (c) If the cluster set of the node becomes null, the node changes its state to *cluster_head*.

(v) Contention between the Cluster Heads is resolved by the Least ID method. This is because the Cluster Head does not monitor the cluster.

(vi) An *ordinary_node* receiving packets from more than one *cluster_head* enters into *gw_ready* (gateway ready) state.

(vii) A *gw_ready* node becomes a *gateway* based on the *Intelligent Gateway Selection Heuristic*.

(viii) A *gateway* on receiving packets from other *gateway* or *gw_ready* nodes may change its state based on *Intelligent Gateway Selection Heuristic*.

(ix) If an *ordinary_node* hears from another *ordinary_node* or *dist_gw* of another cluster, and if there are no gateways in the intersection area, it becomes a Distributed Gateway (*dist_gw*).

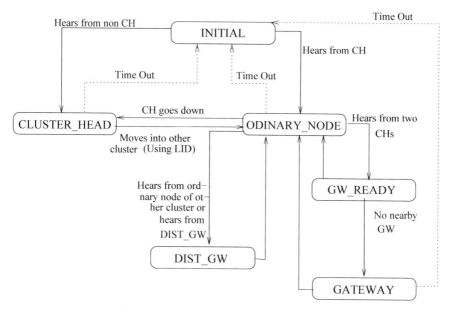

Fig. 9.6 State diagram of efficient passive clustering algorithm

(x) If a *dist_gw* hears from *gateway* or *gw_ready* of the same cluster-pair, it becomes *ordinary_node*.

(xi) No node remains in the intermediate state for a long time.

(xii) If the node times out (using *Special Time-out Mechanism*), its state is set to *initial*.

The nodes change their states based on the status of the last sending node. A node increments its Competition Count whenever it enters into gateway selection process. Unlike the role played by the Cluster Head in other prevailing clustering algorithms, the Cluster Head does not monitor the cluster and it does not contain any extra information. The Cluster Head is different from the other nodes; in that, only the cluster head has the privilege to rebroadcast. The Cluster Head does not monitor the cluster members. If it does, it may become a bottleneck in the cluster architecture. There is an intermediate gateway ready state (*gw_ready*), which reduces the chances of more than one node becoming *gateway* between the same clusters. Figure 9.6 shows the state diagram of Efficient Passive Clustering Algorithm.

9.5.1 Intelligent Gateway Selection Heuristic

Gateways are the intermediate nodes that connect clusters and they have the ability to rebroadcast. The number of rebroadcasts is directly proportional to the number of gateways. Redundant gateways increase the number of rebroadcasts. This is undesirable in WSNs because of the limited bandwidth, power, and Qos constraints. Hence selection of an optimal number of gateways is very essential. Here, we give a heuristic that selects an optimum number of gateways. The original Passive Clustering algorithm selects gateways using the Least_ID principle. This means whenever there is a contention, the one with the lesser ID wins. This method does not consider the topological situation at the time of the decision.

Given that the nodes are mobile, there is a high probability that well-connected gateways will lose their *gateway* status when they compete against the ones having Least_ID. Also, simulation results show that there are generally four or five clusters sharing the same gateway in a dense Wireless Sensor Network. It would be disadvantageous to lose such a well-connected gateway. The Intelligent Gateway Selection Heuristic takes into account the history of competitions a node underwent using Competition Count (C_c) while deciding its status. The Competition Count (C_c) of a node is the number of times a node competes for the *gateway* status. It is set to zero, each time a node acquires either *initial* or Cluster Head status.

Sometimes, it may be necessary to incorporate redundant gateways between clusters in a mobile network. This may be done to ease the traffic flow between clusters to control congestion. This is done by setting the Redundancy Factor (R_f) to a higher value. The Redundancy Factor (R_f) of the network is the maximum number of common clusters that any two neighboring gateways can connect. Since competing gateways can hear each other, they will not compete until the number of gateways in the intersection area is greater than the Redundancy Factor (R_f). Thus, there is a trade-off between optimal connectivity and congestion in Wireless Sensor Networks. For a thin backbone wireless network, Redundancy Factor (R_f) must be set to 1.

To accommodate this heuristic, the information about cluster set of the node (i.e., the set of clusters to which it belongs in case of gateways and distributed gateways), *id* of the node, type of the node, and NOC (size of cluster set) are included in both the packets and the nodes. Competition Count (C_c) and Redundancy Factor (R_f) have to be set in the individual nodes in the WSN. Competition Count (C_c) is reset as soon as the node takes up the *initial* or the Cluster Head state. It is used only when the node is in the other states. It does not make the algorithm inefficient when there is mobility in the network because when a gateway goes far away from the clusters due to its movement, it has a high probability of acquiring either the *initial* or the Cluster Head state. And, the process starts all over again. The heuristic is divided into four cases. In the gateway selection process, these cases do not occur simultaneously.

Case 1: Only node in the intersection area: When the node receives packets from two cluster heads, it enters into the *gw_ready* state and it becomes a gateway.

Case 2: Two or more nodes in the region of intersection of clusters: When a node receives packets from the other Gateway or *gw_ready*, it compares the cardinality of its cluster set with that of the sending node. If both the sets are equal, then the one with the least ID becomes the gateway.

Case 3: The cluster-set of one node in the intersection area is a subset of the cluster-set of another node: Suppose there are two nodes in the intersection area of clusters such that the cluster-set of one node is a subset of the cluster-set of another node. Then the node with the superset will be selected as the gateway. Every gateway performs this comparison by intercepting the packets from its neighboring gateways.

Case 4: When two nodes such that cluster-set(node1)~cluster-set(node2)≠0: In this case, both the nodes have a tendency to declare themselves as gateways when they receive packets from each other. But this may not be optimal, since there may be a difference of just one cluster between the cluster-sets. This leads to the creation of redundant gateways. Clusters are said to possess redundant Gateways, when a cluster is connected to its neighboring cluster by more than one Gateway. The receiving node computes the number of clusters that are common to both the sending node's and receiving node's cluster-sets. If this value is less than or equal to the Redundancy Factor (R_f), then both nodes are designated as Gateways. Otherwise, the node with the least Competition Count (C_c) is designated as the Gateway.

The logic is that, if a node has competed at least once, then there must be one more node in that intersection area, which is capable of covering most of the clusters the former node could connect to. Thus, the other node is given a chance to become a Gateway and extend the connectivity. This heuristic is adaptable to the changes in network topology and network density. The heuristic intelligently selects the best gateway in the intersection area of the two or more clusters.

For instance, in Fig. 9.3, consider the following gateways and their cluster-sets: $G_1(1, 2, 3, 4, 5)$, $G_2(2, 3, 4, 5, 6)$, $G_3(3, 4, 5, 6, 7)$, $G_4(4, 5, 6, 7, 8)$, and $G_5(5, 6, 7, 8, 9)$. If the gateway redundancy factor, R_f is set to 1, only G_1 and G_5 remain as gateways because there is only one cluster common between their cluster-sets ($R_f = 1$). Otherwise, all five would be chosen as gateways. Therefore, there is a reduction in the number of gateways by three. We analyze the proposed heuristics and prove that the heuristics are optimal. And we also analyze the time complexities of our algorithm.

Lemma 1: The EPC algorithm maintains connectivity.
Proof: The number of gateways selected by the EPC algorithm is optimal, since it satisfies the following conditions.

(i) Only one gateway is selected between each cluster pair, unless there is a loss of critical path between a cluster pair. According to *Case 1* and *Case 2* when the cluster sets of more than one node are same, only one of them is selected as the gateway. Also, according to *Case 3* when the cluster set of one node is a subset of the cluster set of the other node, the node having the superset as the cluster set is elected as a gateway.

(ii) At least one gateway is selected between each cluster pair, unless there is no node common to both the clusters.

According to the *Cases 1, 2, and 3* at most one node is selected between cluster pairs. *Case 4* guarantees that optimal number of gateways are chosen between overlapping clusters, by setting the Redundancy Factor (R_f) to a suitable value.

Lemma 2: Number of gateways selected by our algorithm is minimal when $R_f = 1$.
Proof: This is proved by contradiction. Assume that there are two or more gateways between two clusters. If this happens, then the Gateway Selection Heuristic will

ensure that only one of competing gateways retains the *gateway* status as R_f is set to 1. A distributed gateway is selected between a cluster pair only when there is no node in the intersection area of the clusters. Thus, minimum number of gateways are selected to maintain overall connectivity. Because of the nature of passive clustering, more than one node can become gateway simultaneously. But, this situation is overcome by using an intermediate state, between ordinary and gateway states, known as *gw_ready*. A node in *gw_ready* state changes its status to *initial*, if it receives packets from another gateway.

Time Complexity:

When each node receives the packets from at least one of its neighbors, the network becomes stable. The time taken in the worst case is $O(L + Avg\_neighbor)$, where L is the diameter of the network, and $Avg\_neighbor$ is the average number of neighbors of each node. The time complexity of our algorithm is $O(N)$.

9.5.2 Time-out Mechanism

There is no special thread for implementation of time-out mechanism in the nodes and the system clocks of all the nodes need not be synchronized. Every node calculates the time interval between reception of successive packets, asynchronously. If this interval is greater than Time-out, the node goes into the *initial* state and it clears all the stored information. This recalculation and re-clustering is significant as the node may have been isolated for a long time. It may be necessary to change its state relative to its immediate neighbors.

The algorithm provides solutions to all the problems mentioned in the previous section. The solution for the movement of ordinary nodes and gateways is to allow the gateways to send periodic messages to all the cluster heads to check whether the cluster heads have moved. If not, the information corresponding to each non-existing cluster head is removed from the node's cluster table. This will change the status of the sending node, which is desirable. Although control packets are used, they are restricted to gateways only and specifically for collecting information about cluster heads. So, exchanging a small number of control packets does not disturb the passiveness of the algorithm. The advantages gained through incorporating this flexibility in passive clustering are significant. Especially, if the clustering is built on *reactive* protocols like AODV, there is no need to send *hello packets*. There is no way to avoid the formation of redundant clusters during the initial setup. But once this happens, clusters are reformed by making use of the EPC algorithm. The algorithm reduces the number of clusters and also makes each of the clusters thus formed, more stable. A special time-out mechanism is used to solve the problem of cluster head moving out of the cluster.

9.6 Performance Analysis

Passive clustering is simulated in the *ns*-2 simulation environment. The efficiency of the EPC algorithm in reducing the number of rebroadcasts is illustrated. Simulation results reveal that there is a reduction in the control overhead by the application of EPC algorithm. Also, the number of gateways and the number of cluster heads are reduced. The IEEE 802.11 DCF and two-ray propagation model is employed for simulation. The broadcast range for each node is 250 meters. Both the simple passive clustering and improved passive clustering algorithm are implemented on AODV.

By employing the efficient gateway selection heuristic, with the Redundancy Factor set to one, a minimal number of gateways are chosen. Not more than one gateway is chosen between two clusters. The gateways form a *thinner* backbone while maintaining the connectivity among all the clusters within the designated area.

Also, inclusion of more nodes will not increase the number of clusters and the number of gateways will remain fairly constant. Hence, the gateway curve of our algorithm is linear compared to that of the simple passive clustering as shown in Fig. 9.7. The EPC algorithm forms and reforms the clusters in such a way that there will be no two cluster heads that are reachable in one hop. This reduces the number of cluster heads and thus reducing the number of overlapped clusters in the wireless sensor network. Figure 9.8 shows that the EPC algorithm reduces the number of cluster heads compared to simple passive clustering.

The Number of Rebroadcasted Packets (NRP) is the total number of packets that are broadcast and rebroadcast from all the nodes, irrespective of their states. This is a very important parameter because an increase in NRP results in the broadcast storm. The number of rebroadcasts is directly proportional to the total number of cluster

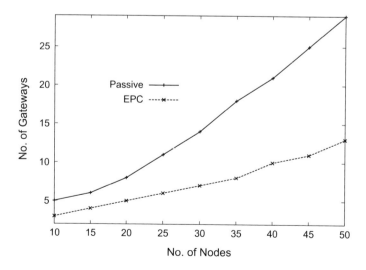

Fig. 9.7 No. of gateways versus no. of nodes

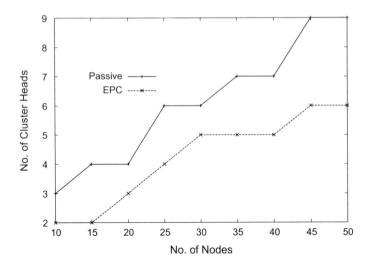

Fig. 9.8 No. of cluster heads versus no. of nodes

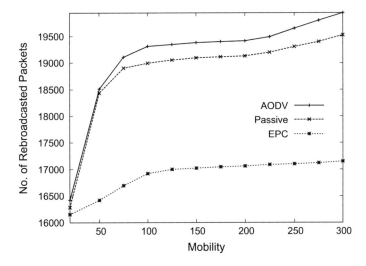

Fig. 9.9 No. of rebroadcasted packets versus mobility

heads, gateways, and distributed gateways in the wireless network. This is because in passive clustering, only the cluster heads, gateways, and distributed gateways of a cluster have the privilege to forward the packets they receive. As depicted in Fig. 9.9, the number of rebroadcasts is the lowest for EPC. With the application of the gateway selection heuristic and other improvements over passive clustering, the number of rebroadcasts is reduced considerably. The curve corresponding to our EPC algorithm is more stable (flatter) than others. The number of rebroadcasts is the highest for AODV since every node forwards the incoming packets. The number

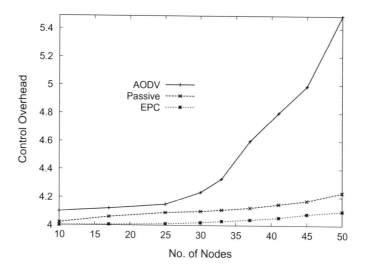

Fig. 9.10 Control overhead versus no. of nodes

of rebroadcast messages in passive clustering is lower than AODV, but much higher than EPC, and obtain better QoS in the network.

As Fig. 9.10 shows, in the EPC algorithm, control packets are employed only by the gateways. Even though we are using explicit control messages, the result of these messages is to make the clustering much more stable and hence reduce the control messages. Thus, the total control overhead of the EPC algorithm is lower than the other cases. In passive clustering, there are no explicit control packets, but the clustering mechanism reduces the generation of control packets. The control overhead is higher than the EPC algorithm. The control overhead curve for AODV is steep, since every node sends control packets to its neighbors and as the number of nodes increase, the number of control packets also rises exponentially.

9.7 Summary

The simulation results show that the EPC Algorithm is inexpensive, efficient, and stable. The number of clusters is found to be optimal in dense wireless sensor networks. This work has proved that Passive Clustering becomes practically possible by implementing the intelligent gateway selection heuristic and on-demand timeout mechanism. Frequent changes in cluster architecture are avoided by precluding repeated re-election of cluster heads. This improves the QoS network performance. Future work can be carried out by employing distributed gateways to route packets.

References

1. C.R. Lin, M. Gerla, Adaptive clustering for mobile wireless networks. In: IEEE J. Select. Areas Commun. 1265–1275 (1996)
2. Y. Yi, M. Gerla, T.-J. Kwon, *Efficient flooding in Ad Hoc networks using on-demand (passive) cluster formation* (Proc, MobiHoc, 2002)
3. F. Dai, J. Wu, Distributed dominant pruning in Ad hoc wireless networks. Florida Atlantic University, Technical Report TR-CSE-FAU-02-02 (2002)
4. A.A. Abbasi, M. Younis, A survey on clustering algorithms for wireless sensor networks. Comput. Commun. **30**(14), 2826–2841 (2007)
5. Y.-C. Tseng, S.-Y. Ni, Y.-S. Chen, J.-P. Sheu, The broadcast storm problem in a mobie Ad Hoc network, in *Proceedings of the Mobicom* (1999)
6. Y.-C. Tseng, S.-Y. Ni, E.-Y. Shih, Adaptive approaches to relieving broadcast storms in a wireless multihop mobile Ad Hoc network, in *Infocom* (2001)
7. A. Qayyum, L. Viennot, A. Laouiti, Multipoint relaying: an efficient technique for flooding in mobile wireless networks, in *INRIA Report* (2000)
8. H. Lim, C. Kim, *Flooding in wireless Ad hoc networks* (IEEE Comput, Commun, 2000)
9. W. Lou, J. Wu, On reducing broadcast redundancy in Ad hoc wireless networks. IEEE Trans. Mob. Comput. **1**(2), 111–123 (2002)
10. A.D. Amis, R. Prakash, T.H.P. Voung, D.T. Huynh, Max-min D-cluster formation in wireless Ad Hoc networks, in *IEEE INFOCOM* (2000)
11. P. Gupta, P.R. Kumar, The capacity of wireless networks. IEEE Trans. Inform. Theory **46**, 388–404 (2000)
12. M. Grossglauser, D.N.C. Tse, Mobility increases the capacity of Ad Hoc wireless networks, in *IEEE/ACM Transactions on Networking*, vol. 10 (2002)
13. V. Bhargavan, B. Das, Routing in Ad Hoc networks using minimum connected dominating sets, in *International Conference on Communications'97* (1997)
14. B. Das, R. Shivakumar, V. Bhargavan, Routing in Ad Hoc networks using a spine, in *International Conference on Computers and Communication Networks'97* (1997)
15. R. Shivakumar, B. Das, V. Bhargavan, An improved spine-based infrastructure for routing in Ad Hoc networks, in *IEEE Symposium on Computers and Communication Networks'98* (1998)
16. P.-j. Wan, K.M. Alzoubi, O. Frieder, Distributed construction of connected dominating set in wireless Ad Hoc networks, in *Proceedigs of IEEE INFOCOM '02* (Chicago, USA, 2002)
17. M.V. Marathe, H. Breu, H.B. Hunt III, S.S. Ravi, D.J. Rosenkrantz, *Simple Heuristics for Unit Disk Graph* (Addison-Wesley, Narosa, 1995)
18. M. Gerla, J.T.-C. Tsai, Multicluster, mobile, multimedia radio network. ACM J. Wirel. Netw. **1**(3), 255–265 (1995)
19. K. Gilhousen, I.M. Jacobs et al., On the capacity of a cellular CDAM system. IEEE Trans. Vehicul. Technol. 303–312 (1991)
20. A. Ephremides, J. E. Wieselthier, D.J. Baker, A design concept for reliable mobile radio networks with frequency hopping signaling, in *Proceedings of the IEEE* (1991), pp. 56–73
21. C.C. Chiang, H.K. Wu, W. Liu, M. Gerla, Routing in clustered multihop, mobile wireless networks with fading channel, in *The Proceedings of the IEEE Singapore International Conference on Networks* (1996), pp. 197–211
22. B. Williams, T. Camp, *Comparison of broadcasting techniques for mobile Ad Hoc networks, in Proceedings of the MOBIHOC'02* (Colorado School of Mines, Golden, Colorado, 2000)
23. D.B. Johnson, D.A. Maltz, Dynamic source routing in Ad Hoc networks. Mob. Comput. 153–181 (1996)
24. C. Perkins, E. Royer, S. Das, *Ad hoc on Demand Distance Vector (AODV) Routing* (Internet draft, IETF, 1999)
25. R.C. Jin, T. Gao, J.Y. Song, J.Y. Zou, L.D. Wang, Passive cluster-based multipath routing protocol for wireless sensor networks. Wirel. Netw. **19**(8), 1851–1866 (2013)
26. Y. Liu, N. Xiong, Y. Zhao, A.V. Vasilakos, J. Gao, Y. Jia, Multi-layer clustering routing algorithm for wireless vehicular sensor networks. IET Commun. **4**(7), 810–816 (2010)

27. M. Chen, V.C. Leung, S. Mao, Y. Yuan, Directional geographical routing for real-time video communications in wireless sensor networks. Comput. Commun. **30**(17), 3368–3383 (2007)
28. Y. Xiao, M. Peng, J. Gibson, G.G. Xie, D.Z. Du, A.V. Vasilakos, Tight performance bounds of multihop fair access for MAC protocols in wireless sensor networks and underwater sensor networks. IEEE Trans. Mob. Comput. **11**(10), 1538–1554 (2012)
29. T.J. Kwon, M. Gerla, V.K. Varma, M. Barton, T.R. Hsing, Efficient flooding with passive clustering-an overhead-free selective forward mechanism for Ad hoc/sensor networks. Proc. IEEE **91**(8), 1210–1220 (2003)
30. W. Wang, F. Du, Q. Xu, An improvement of LEACH routing protocol based on trust for wireless sensor networks, in *5th International Conference on Wireless Communications, Networking and Mobile Computing* (2009), pp. 1–4
31. G. Liu, C. Wei, A new multi-path routing protocol based on cluster for underwater acoustic sensor networks, in *2011 International Conference on Multimedia Technology* (2011), pp. 91–94
32. X.C. Lu, H.Y. An, Y.X. Peng, W. Peng, A cluster-based QoS multipath routing protocol for large-scale MANET. Ruan Jian Xue Bao (J. Softw.) **18**(7), 1786–1798 (2007)
33. Y. Jing, X. Mai, X. Jinfu, X. Baoguo, H. Lu, A cluster-based multipath delivery scheme for wireless sensor networks, in *2nd IEEE International Conference on Broadband Network Multimedia Technology* (2009), pp. 286–291
34. A. Bhatia, P. Kaushik, A cluster based minimum battery cost AODV routing using multipath route for Zigbee, in *2008 16th IEEE International Conference on Networks* (2008), pp. 1–7
35. Z. Bidai, H. Haffaf, M. Maimour, Node disjoint multi-path routing for ZigBee cluster-tree wireless sensor networks, in *2011 International Conference on Multimedia Computing and Systems* (2011), pp. 1–6
36. I.T. Almalkawi, M. Guerrero Zapata, J.N. Al-Karaki, A secure cluster-based multipath routing protocol for WMSNs. Sensors **11**(4), 4401–4424 (2011)
37. A.S. Hafid, F. Chender, T.J. Kwon, Energy aware passive clustering in wireless mobile networks. in *2008 International Wireless Communications and Mobile Computing Conference* (2008), pp. 535–540
38. S. Bandyopadhyay, E.J. Coyle, Minimizing communication costs in hierarchically-clustered networks of wireless sensors. Comput. Netw. **44**(1), 1–16 (2004)
39. D.E. Knuth, *Fundamental Algorithms* (Addison-Wesley, Narosa, 1985)

Chapter 10
SAAQ: Secure Aggregation for Approximate Queries in WSNs

Abstract Wireless Sensor Networks are vulnerable to communication failures and security attacks. Multipath based aggregation techniques such as synopsis diffusion are proposed to address communication failures. This chapter proposes Secure Aggregation for Approximate Queries in Wireless Sensor Networks (SAAQ) where Message Authentication Codes (MACs) are transmitted along with the synopses that are generated using primitive polynomials. SAAQ ensures data freshness and integrity at a communication cost of $O(1)$. Simulation results show that the SAAQ protocol results in lower energy consumption and communication and computation cost compared to the state-of-art protocols [1, 2].

10.1 Introduction

Wireless Sensor Networks (WSNs) consist of sensors that generally sense that are severely constrained in resources such as energy, bandwidth, memory, and processing capacity. The maximum energy consuming task of a sensor node is Message transmission. Hence the network lifetime decreases with the number of transmissions. In-network aggregation techniques that combine partial results at intermediate nodes can significantly reduce the number of transmissions and increase the network lifetime. The network topology can be cluster-based or tree-based both of which are vulnerable to communication failures. Later multipath routing techniques were introduced that allow a node to have multiple parents in the aggregation hierarchy. Multipath routing incurs message duplication that leads to over counting in the case of duplicate-sensitive aggregates, such as *Count* and *Sum*.

To address the issue of over counting in multipath aggregation two approaches could be applied: synopsis diffusion that uses a bit-vector named synopsis to repre-

©2006 IEEE. Reprinted, with permission, from Proceedings of the International Conference on Data Science and Engineering ICDSE'16, E. G. Prathima, T. S. Prakash, K. R. Venugopal, S. S. Iyengar and L. M. Patnaik, SADA: Secure approximate data aggregation in Wireless Sensor Networks, pp. 1–6
Reprinted by permission from International Journal of Information Processing, Volume 10, Issue 1, Copyright 2016.

sent the single sensor reading or a partial aggregates based on on Flajolet–Martin's counting sketches approach. But *Sketches* return approximate results to the query due to multipath propagation of results. WSNs are vulnerable to various types of security attacks due to the inherent broadcast nature of radio communication. Hence security must be provided while performing aggregation. Many types of attacks can be launched on in-network aggregation such as compromising a node to affect aggregated results, impersonating a node, and replaying an outdated message. There is a necessity of secure data aggregation.

Performing secure data aggregation is challenging due to the following reasons: (1) Most of the security protocols encrypt and authenticate data before transmission and decrypt it at the Base Station whereas data aggregation protocols apply aggregation function on plain text data. (2) Data aggregation alters the data and hence it is difficult to provide source authentication and data authentication.

10.2   Related Works

10.2.1   Routing and Data Aggregation

Considine et al. [3] investigated the use of approximate in-network aggregation for computing duplicate-sensitive aggregates by combining duplicate-insensitive *sketches* with multipath routing techniques. The sketches generated are compressed using run-length encoding and reduces the space requirement by 30%.

Nath et al. [2] presented synopsis diffusion, a general framework to overcome double-counting problem where best effort, multipath routing schemes called rings are used together with order and duplicate-insensitive (ODI) synopsis. The implicit acknowledgment mechanism enables synopsis diffusion to adapt to dynamic message loss condition. In [4], the shortcomings of *sum* and *count* queries in [2] have been addressed by applying synopsis diffusion for other aggregation functions, uniform sample, and Top-k items. This algorithm is light-weight to monitor and is energy efficient. For certain aggregation queries, synopsis diffusion can return only approximate answer.

Fan and Chen [5] proposed linear counting sketches for multipath routing based in-network aggregation. The algorithm involves low computational cost and low sketch space when compared to existing sketches. In this approach, LC-sketches are assumed to be of fixed size and nodes at high level send sketches with most entries zero that leads to wastage of energy. To deal with the over counting problem, two algorithms based on linear counting techniques were proposed in [6] namely Robust In-network Aggregation using LC-Sketches (RIA-LC) and Robust In-network Aggregation using Dynamic Counting Sketches (RIA-DC). Sensor nodes adaptively determine the space for the sketches in RIA-DC technique and hence outperforms the RIA-LC scheme which preallocates LC sketch space in most cases. The Scalable Counting (SC) sketch and its variant adaptive scalable counting (ASC) sketch presented in [7] can produce duplicate-insensitive synopsis and at the same time, suppress data transmissions insignificant to aggregate computation. This algorithm performs in-network aggregation with much less space requirement than [6]. Tarannum et al. [8], Manjula et al. [9], Kanavalli et al. [10], and Prathap et al. [11] proposed Energy-Efficient Routing Protocol that can significantly improve the network lifetime.

10.2.2 Secure Data Aggregation

Yang et al. [12] developed a novel secured diffusion that uses localized location-binding keys for both neighbor and node-to-sink authentication. The sink selects a high-quality path to the neighbors based on data authenticity and quality. Yu et al. [13] proposed that Verifiable Aggregate Synopsis (VAS) manipulated readings do not contribute to the final aggregate. The communication overhead is reduced by using broadcast sampling protocol that produces multiplicative-ϵ approximate of the predicate count or sum. The keyed predicate test of broadcast sampling protocol makes it resilient to DoS attack. VAS verifies individual one bit in the final synopsis and incurs additional computation overhead.

Garofalakis et al. [14] derived proof sketches that provide verifiable approximations for a broad class of distributed queries. It combines Flajolet–Martin (FM) sketches with authentication manifests resulting in low false negative rate. The algorithm is robust as the adversary must compromise the aggregators near the root of the topology to get near the worst case bounds undetected.

Nath et al. [15] developed Secure Outsourced Aggregation (SECOA) for aggregation by untrusted third-party service providers based on unified use of one-way chain and supports a wide range of aggregation functions. The proposed framework detects malicious aggregators without communicating with sensors and incurs low additional communication and computational overheads.

Yang et al. [16] have designed a Secure Hop-by-hop Data Aggregation Protocol (SDAP) that uses a probabilistic grouping to partition the aggregation tree into subtrees of similar size. A commit-based hop-by-hop aggregation is performed to generate group aggregate and is verified by the base station. The protocol effectively defends against both count and value changing attacks.

Roy et al. [17] presented a data aggregation protocol for *sum* and *count* aggregates that secures the original synopsis diffusion protocol by sending Message Authentication Code (MAC)s to the base station with partial results computed at each level in the hierarchy. The base station can detect the presence of false sub-aggregates by verifying these MACs. The Verification Algorithm [18] provides better security by verifying the aggregate and ensures that it does not have any false contribution. A two-phase attack resilient protocol [1] has been proposed by which the base station is able to calculate the correct aggregate even in presence of falsified sub-aggregate attack. The proposed algorithm computes a MAC for each of the '1' bit it is contributing and incurs increased communication overhead and latency.

10.2.3 Introduction to Synopsis Diffusion Framework

In Synopsis Diffusion framework [2], nodes organize themselves into rings around the base station, called *adaptive rings*, when the query propagates through the network. This topology is called adaptive rings because nodes create their neighbor list during each query dissemination phase and hence do not have *failed* nodes in their neighbor list. A node X is in ring L_i, if it is i hops away from base station. A node in ring L_i has multiple parents in ring L_{i-1} and multiple children in ring L_{i+1}.

Once the query is received by all the leaf nodes (in outermost ring), the aggregation process starts from outermost ring. Each node X in the outermost ring computes synopsis representing its data by applying synopsis generation function and then broadcasts its synopsis LS_X. The synopsis is a bit-vector which is generated using Probabilistic Counting with Stochastic Averaging (PCSA) algorithm proposed by Flajolet–Martin [19]. Each node computes m synopses for it's reading V_X, from which one synopsis is selected randomly for transmission.

A node Y in the inner ring first generates its local synopsis by applying *SynGen()* and waits for synopsis from its children. When a node Y at level L_i receives the synopsis from a node X in level L_{i-1}, it performs aggregation by applying *SynFuse()* function as shown below:

$$FS_Y = LS_Y | FS_{X_1} | FS_{X_2} | ... | FS_{X_c}$$

Where FS_{Id} is the fused synopsis of the node Id, LS_Y is the synopsis generated at node Y corresponding to its data V_Y, and c represents the number of children of node Y. The node Y then broadcasts the fused synopsis FS_Y. This process is repeated until all the aggregated synopses reach the base station. A node broadcasts its synopsis multiple times to provide better resilience against communication failure.

The base station fuses all received synopses. The final synopsis obtained after *SynFuse()* [2] is a bit-vector that is represented by the regular expression, $1^{z-1}0[101]^{l-z}$ where z is the index of leftmost (least significant) 0-bit in the final synopsis. Finally, the base station applies synopsis evaluation function *SynEval()*. *SynEval()* for count query is expressed as $2^z/0.7735$, since E(Z), expectation of index of least significant 0 bit, Z is $\approx log_2(\phi N)$ where $\phi \approx 0.78$. *SynEval()* for Sum query is expressed as 2^z.

10.2.4 Secured Data Aggregation

Message Authentication Codes provide a means for ensuring data integrity. MAC is a one-way transformation of the data and shared secret key. Roy et al. [1] have used MACs to secure the original synopsis discussion technique. Each node in the network shares a pairwise key with the base station (sink). After generating reading, the sensor node generates a synopsis representing its reading. The node then generates a MAC authenticating each of the 1 bit it is contributing.

Suppose if there are k 1s in the synopsis generated at node X and let $I_1, I_2, ..., I_k$ represent the index of the first 1 bit, second 1 bit, and so on. Then k MACs are generated authenticating each of the indices $I_1, I_2, ..., I_k$. Let M_j represent the MAC corresponding to I_j, then M_j is computed as $<X, V_X, K_X, I_j, \text{Seed}> \, \forall j = 1$ to k, as input.

The node X transmits the tuple $<X, V_X, FS_X, I_1, I_2, ..., I_k, M_1, M_2, ..., M_k >$ where V_X is the reading of node X and FS_X is the aggregated synopsis. A node may transmit a MAC M_j that is either generated by itself or received from one of its children. At the base station, all synopsis received are fused. Then each MAC M_j received corresponding to index I_j that is 1 in the fused synopsis is verified. If an index I_j is not verified, then the base station initiates the second phase of verification where each node sends all MACs for index I_j that is received from its children including its own to the base station. There are three main issues with this approach:

(1) If a node launches an inflation attack by injecting 1 in place of 0 in the synopsis, its parent may generate a genuine MAC authenticating this false one and transmit it, the attack will remain undetected. (2) If an inflation attack is launched, the size of message increases resulting in an overall increase in communication overhead and energy consumption. (3) The MAC received at base station may be generated by a node at any level of hierarchy, so base station should perform a trial and error using each (id, key) pair to verify a MAC.

10.3   Problem Definition and Models

Given a sensor network G, with N sensor nodes and a query Q issued from the base station, compute duplicate-sensitive aggregate corresponding to the query Q on demand, while removing contributions from the malicious nodes, M at a reduced communication and computation overhead.

Let D_i be the data generated at ith sensor node and let $M = m_1, m_2, ..., m_k$ be the contribution from k malicious nodes, then the computed aggregate A for the query Q is given as

$$A_Q(G) = \sum_{i=1}^{n} D_i - \sum_{j=1}^{k} m_j$$

where,

$D_i = C_i; \; \forall i \in L : C_i = 1$ for count query,

$D_i = S_i; \; \forall i \in L : S_i = V_i; V_i$ is the reading of ith sensor node , for the sum query, and

$D_i = (C_i, S_i)$ for the average query.

Here L is a set of leaf nodes.

Objectives:
1. Reduce malicious contribution.
2. Reduce communication cost.
3. Improve the QoS of the Network.
3. Increase network lifetime.

10.3.1   Network Model

The Sensor Network consists of N homogeneous having a communication and computation capabilities similar to that of MicaZ or Telos. The sensor network is organized into a 2D grid of size $L \times L$ as shown in Fig. 10.1. The sensor nodes send their data to the sink through multi-hop transmission. All the nodes in the network are assumed to be loosely synchronized. Every node in the network has the same initial energy E_0.

Extended adaptive rings: SAAQ uses extended version of adaptive rings topology. This architecture allows a node at level L to have parents in the same level in addition to parents in level L-1(previous level). The aggregation time is divided into $n - 1$ mini-slots, where n is the maximum number of neighbors a node has in the previous level. All odd numbered nodes transmit in odd numbered mini-slots and all even numbered nodes transmit in even numbered slots. In adaptive rings topology as shown in Fig. 10.1, every node in the four corners of each ring has only one parent. So if the data from a corner node is lost, it cannot be aggregated.

The extended adaptive rings allow the nodes to have parents in the same level and in the previous level. The nodes in the corner (odd numbered nodes) transmit in the odd numbered mini-slot. Data from such nodes is to be gathered and aggregated by neighboring nodes in the same level and the previous level. The extended adaptive

Fig. 10.1 Deployment of
sensor nodes in 4 × 4 grid

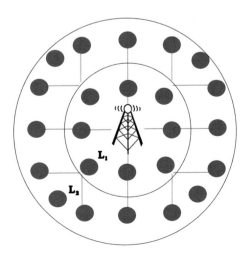

rings are shown in Fig. 10.1. The nodes that have not yet transmitted their synopsis, i.e., with unexpired timer, aggregate the received data from neighbors in the same level before transmitting. Extended adaptive rings ensure that data of each node is aggregated by at least 3 neighbors and hence it is more resilient to failures than adaptive rings.

10.3.2 Attack Model

It is assumed the sink cannot be compromised whereas all other sensor nodes are assumed to be vulnerable to attacks. SAAQ algorithm tries to address mainly two types of attacks, replay attack and false data injection (Fig. 10.2).

Replay attack: Replay attack affects data freshness. Here a compromised node retransmits a genuine synopsis packet that has been generated during one of the previous epochs in place of current synopsis packet.

False data injection: In this type of attack, a compromised node tries to introduce false contribution in its aggregated data. If the data sensed by sensors are transmitted as bit vector (such as synopsis or sketches), a compromised node may either inflate (where bit with value 0 is changed to (1) or deflate (bit with value 1 is converted to 0) either in its own synopsis or aggregated synopsis.

10.3.3 Security Model

Message authentication codes can ensure data integrity. Message Authentication Codes are generated using a cryptographic hash function that takes data, D, and key K as input and generates a message digest. SAAQ assumes that every node X is preloaded with one master key K which is generated at the base station. If a node X wishes to compute MAC for synopsis either self generated or received from its neighbors, it performs a re-keying operation to generate K_X computed as follows:

Fig. 10.2 Malicious node injecting deflation attack

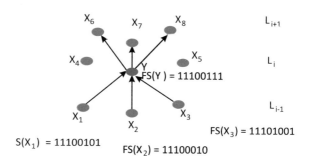

$$K_X = f_K(id,e) = (K\|id\,) \oplus e$$

A new key is generated for every round synopsis that is to be transmitted. This key, K_X is used for computing the Message Authentication Code. Only the master key, K is stored at all the sensor nodes. The key of each node K_X is generated in the MAC generation procedure. Even if an attacker gets the master key, a genuine MAC authenticating fake data cannot be generated. In SAAQ, Pairwise verification is performed at each node using the same MAC generation algorithm. If an index is not verified, then the bit is flipped back to 0.

10.4 The SAAQ Algorithm

SAAQ aims at allowing the base station to obtain the approximate estimate of the aggregate while keeping the computational, communication and memory overhead minimal. For achieving this, SAAQ uses a pull-based architecture for data collection where the sink pulls data from the sensor nodes using a query. SAAQ can be used for both persistent as well as single shot queries. The algorithm comprises of three phases (Algorithm 10.2). The notations used in the Algorithm are given in Table 10.1

(1) Query dissemination: Query propagates through network and Extended adaptive rings are formed,

(2) Synopsis generation and aggregation: Synopsis is generated and aggregated, and

(3) Evaluation.

Table 10.1 List of notations

Notation	Meaning
Id, X, Y	Id of sensor node
L_i	Level of the sensor node with *id i*
V_X	Reading of node X
Q	Query from the base station like sum, count, and average
LS_X	Local synopsis of node X
FS_X	Fused synopsis of node X
$LS[i]$	*i*th bit in the Local synopsis
len	Length of the synopsis (bit vector)
Z	Index of least significant 0 bit in the synopsis
D_i	Data of sensor node *i*
K	Key that is preloaded in all sensor nodes
K_i	Key of sensor node *i*
M_I	MAC authenticating index I in the synopsis

10.4.1 Query Dissemination

In this phase, the Base Station generates two random integers; a random integer g and a prime number p. These two random integers ensure data freshness and are used for exchanging pairwise keys. The base station generates a query packet containing the fields: $< Q, g, p, t, e, L >$, where Q represents the type of query (count, sum, or average), t represents time of query generation, and e represents the interval after which subsequent aggregated data packets are expected. Base station is the only node at level 0, hence when query packet is generated at the base station, it sets L to 0.

When the query packet reaches a node X for the first time, it sets a timer for synopsis generation. The node X then increments the level field *lvl* in the packet by 1 and then sets its own level to $L+1$. The node also stores all information related to the query locally. Then it replaces the *id* field in packet by its own *id* and rebroadcasts the packet. Here limited flooding technique is used to reduce the number of packets in transit. A node X rebroadcasts query packet QP_j for query j, when at least one of the two following conditions hold: (i) QP_j is received for first time at X (ii) QP_j is already received but the level L of X has become $L-1$.

On receipt of query packet, each sensor node updates its active neighbor list. In addition, the node sets a timer inversely proportional to its level, i.e., timer of leaf nodes expire first and timer of nodes at *level 1* expires last. The two random integers p and g allows a node X to differentiate query packet QP_j from the previous query packet QP_{j-1} corresponding to queries Q_i and Q_{i-1}, respectively and hence ensures data freshness.

This process is repeated until the query packet reaches all nodes in the network. The resultant topology formed is the *extended adaptive rings*, presented in Sect. 10.3.

10.4.2 Synopsis Generation and Aggregation

10.4.2.1 Synopsis Generation

When the timer for synopsis generation at node X expires, it generates reading v_X corresponding to the type of query as discussed in Sect. 10.2 and resets the data generation timer. Then node X generates its local synopsis. *Primitive polynomials modulo 2* with coefficients 0 or 1 is used as an alternative to hash function to generate random bit positions. For example, in order to generate random bits for count query, we can use the polynomial $(14 \oplus 5 \oplus 3 \oplus 1 \oplus 0)$ where $\oplus$ performs bitwise XOR on selected bits of input data. The order of the polynomial is chosen to be equal to length of bit-vector *len*.

SAAQ uses *primitive polynomials modulo 2* to generate its local synopsis, corresponding *synGen()* method is shown in Function 10.1. The advantage of using *primitive polynomials modulo 2* as hash function in comparison to PCSA-based hash function is two fold: (1) Since it uses bitwise XOR and shift operations, com-

---

Function 10.1: Function to generate synopsis using primitive polynomials modulo 2

Function: SynGen
Input: Id, V_{Id}, len
Data: qtime $= t + (e * round)$; t is time query generated at base station and e is the interval in which data is expected

1 **if** $Query =$ "Count" **then**

2   Set $rseed$ to $Id \oplus qtime$

3   Initialize i to 0

4   **while** $i < len$ **do**

5   Perform bitwise XOR on $(14 \oplus 5 \oplus 3 \oplus 2 \oplus 0)$ of $rseed$

6   Store result in $newbit$

7   Perform 1 bit Left Shift on $rseed$

8   Reset $rseed$ to $rseed \oplus newbit$

9   **if** $newbit=1$ **then**

10   Set $LS[i]$ to 1

11   increment i

12 **else if** $Query =$ "Sum" **then**

13   Set $n1$ to number of 1 bits in V_{Id}

14   Set rseed to $Id \cdot V_{Id} \oplus qtime$

15   Initialize i to 0

16   Initialize j to 0

17   **while** $i < n1$ **do**

18   **while** $j < len$ **do**

19   Perform bitwise XOR on $(21 \oplus 2 \oplus 0)$ of $rseed$

20   Store result in $newbit$

21   Perform 1 bit Left Shift on $rseed$

22   Reset $rseed$ to $rseed \oplus newbit$

23   **if** $newbit = 1$ **then**

24   Set $LS[j]$ to 1alg:SynGenPP

25   Increment j

putation cost is low (2) It does not require arrays for the computation in comparison to PCSA-based hash function, which uses two arrays of size 64 and hence it incurs very low memory overhead. SynGen function works differently for *Sum* and *Count* queries as shown in Function Algorithm 10.1.

(i) Count Query: Synopsis for count query is simple. As discussed above, the *hash()* function implemented using *primitive polynomials modulo 2* and *CountSyn()* function invokes *hash()* function repeatedly until it returns 1. If *i*th invocation of *hash(id, len)* returns 1, then *i*th bit of its local synopsis LS_{id} is set to 1 as in original synopsis diffusion.

Synopsis Aggregation *(ii) Sum Query:* To generate Synopsis for Sum query, node X executes the *CountSyn()* function *b* number of times and sets, where *b* is the number of 1 bits in reading measured by X. The local synopsis LS_X has *b* bits set to 1.

Let V_{max} represent the maximum value of count, then the number of nodes contributing to *i*th bit of synopsis is equal to $V_{max}/2^i$. Let *c* represent the number of consecutive 1 bits in the synopsis, then $c = z - 1$, where *z* is the index of least significant 0 bit. $E(c) = log_2(V_{max})$.

10.4.2.2 Synopsis Aggregation

MAC generation: MAC generation procedure takes $< id, V, K, FS_{id}, L, g, p, t, e >$ as input. It first generates a key for this data collection round using the common key shared by all nodes using a function similar to Diffie–Hellman Key exchange protocol Key $= ((K \| id) \oplus qtime \oplus g)^{L+L-1}$ mod p, where *g* and *p* are random numbers transmitted along with query from sink. $qtime = t + (e * \text{round})$; *t* and *e* are received at each node along with query and round represents the number of intervals lapsed after receiving the query Q in synopsis generation and aggregation. L_i is the level of sending node.

Once the Key is computed, four MACs are generated using cryptographic hash function authenticating each of the four most significant '1' bit it is contributing. The MAC thus generated is then grouped into 4 byte chunks and then a bitwise XOR operation is performed on each of the 4 byte chunks to obtain the final MAC of size 4 bytes. For example, Let M be the 128 bit MAC generated, then divide M into blocks of size 4 bytes say m_1, m_2, m_3, m_4 and recompute MAC as $M = m_1 \oplus m_2 \oplus m_3 \oplus m_4$. The reason for choosing exactly index of four most significant 1 bits for MAC generation is that the length of the bit vector *len* is chosen to be $log_2(V_{max}) + 4$ where V_{max} represents the maximum value of sum or count. The expected index of the least significant '0' bit E(Z), is at $log_2(V_{max}) + 1$. If an inflation attack is launched at any bit position (index) *i*, it does not affect the value of final approximate computed at base station as long as $i < Z$.

When any non-leaf node X at L_i receives a packet from its neighbor at level L_{i+1}, it first generates MAC for the received synopsis using the MAC generation algorithm discussed above. If the generated MAC agrees with the received MAC, then X aggregates the data received from Y with its own as follows: $FS_X = FS_X | FS_Y$, where | indicates bitwise OR operation.

When timer of X expires, X generates its fused synopsis and then generates four MACs authenticating the four most significant 1 bits it is contributing. It then broadcasts its fused synopsis along with the four MACs and its reading corresponding to query Q_j to P_x.

Evaluation phase is performed at the Sink node. When the sink node receives a data packet from a node at level 1 say Y, it generates four MACs authenticating the index of four rightmost 1 bits using the MAC generation procedure discussed above. It then verifies the received MACs with the generated ones and if they match, then the synopsis in the received packet is fused at the sink as mentioned in Data generation and aggregation above. When the sink receives synopsis from all of its eight neighbors or when its timer expires, the sink starts evaluating fused data. If the query is *Count* or *Sum*, then result it evaluated as $A_Q(G) = \sum_{i=1}^{n} D_i$, where $n <= 8$ (n is number of neighbors excluding malicious nodes). If the query is to compute average, then final result is evaluated as $A_Q(G) = \sum_{i=1}^{n} S_i / \sum_{i=1}^{n} C_i$, where $n <= 8$ (n is number of neighbors excluding malicious nodes)

10.5   Results and Analysis

This section presents a detailed analysis of the simulation results performed on *ns*-2 simulator. The basic network size used consists of 900 sensor nodes placed in a *grid* topology. The sink is placed at the center of the grid as shown in Fig. 10.1. The node density is 4 nodes/m^2. The communication range R is chosen to be $\sqrt{2}$, so that each node in the network has exactly 8 neighbors. Each sensor bears a unique *id* from 1 to 899 and *Id* of the sink node is 0. During each data collection round, every sensor generates its reading which is a random uniform integer within range 0–250.

Performance of SAAQ is compared with that of two-phase verification algorithm (referred as SDA-2PV) proposed by Roy et al. [1] which computes the exact aggregate even in presence of falsified sub-aggregate attack and Synopsis Diffusion algorithm (referred as SynDiff) presented by Nath et al. in [2].

The parameters considered for analysis include *Network Size, Average Energy Dissipated per Node, Average Packet Size:,* and *Root Mean Square Error.* RMS Error is a measure of deviation of computed result at sink from expected value and is computed using the formula

$$RMSError = 1/V \sqrt{(1/r \sum_{i=1}^{r} (V_i - V)^2)}$$

where V_i is the value of result computed at the sink during round i and V is the value of expected result at the sink. The closer the value of RMS error to 0, the accurate is the computed aggregate.

Algorithm 10.2: SAAQ: Secure Aggregation for Approximate Queries in Wireless Sensor Networks

---

Input : Query Packet *QPacket*$_t$
Output: Aggregated sum or count A_Q

1 **begin**

3 | **PHASE I: Query dissemination**

4 | **if** *Level of received QPacket$_t$+1 < Level of X* **then**

5 | | **if** *QPacket$_t$ is received for the first time* **then**

6 | | | Set Data generation timer

7 | | Increment *level* field in *QPacket$_t$* by 1

8 | | Set Level of *X* to *level* field of *QPacket$_t$*

9 | | Set *Id* field of *QPacket$_t$* to *X*

10 | | Start aggregation Timer $\propto 1/L$

11 | **PHASE II: Synopsis Generation and Aggregation**

12 | Generate *LS* using Function 10.1

13 | Initialize *FS* to *LS*

14 | **foreach** *DPacket Received* **do**

15 | | **if** *Level of received DPacket $\geq$ level of X* **then**

16 | | | Generate MACs authenticating index *I* of 4 most significant 1 bits in received Synopsis

17 | | | **foreach** *MAC M$_I$* **do**

18 | | | | **if** *Received MAC is verified* **then**

20 | | | | | Retain the 1 bit in received synopsis

21 | | | | **else**

22 | | | | | Flip the bit to 0

23 | | | Aggregate the synopsis in received packet

24 | | Update active neighbor list

25 | **if** *Aggregation timer fires* **then**

26 | | Generate MACs authenticating index *I* of 4 most significant 1 bits of aggregated synopsis

27 | | Create data packet *DPacket* containing, reading synopsis and four MACs

28 | | Broadcast *DPacket*

29 | **PHASE III: Evaluation**

30 | Find index of least significant 0 bit *Z*

31 | Compute A_Q as 2^Z

10.5.1   Energy Consumption per Data Collection Round

The main source of energy loss in sensor nodes is data communication. More precisely transmission consumes more energy in comparison with reception. Figure 10.3 shows average energy expended in transmission without any attack. The average energy dissipation of SADA is least among the three algorithms due to extended adaptive rings. The extended adaptive ring uses TDMA where nodes adjacent nodes transmit their data in alternate time slots. But in adaptive rings, all the nodes in the same ring transmit multiple number of times simultaneously to provide resilience to communication failure. This retransmission increase the communication cost and hence the energy consumed. SynDiff consumes the least energy in comparison to SADA and SDA-2PV. The smaller the size of synopsis packet, the lesser the energy consumption. The energy consumed is uniform throughout its operation.

10.5.2   Impact of Inflation Attack on Final Aggregate Computed

Figure 10.4 shows the impact of the percentage of compromised nodes over the Root Mean Square (RMS) error. As the number of compromised nodes increases, RMS Error also increases. The lower the value of RMS Error, the better the performance of the algorithm. Out of the three algorithms, Syndiff is most susceptible to inflation

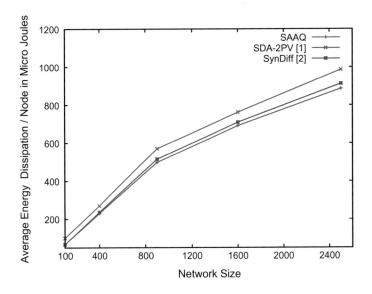

Fig. 10.3 Energy consumption per data collection round in absence of attack

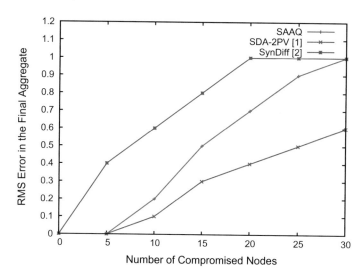

Fig. 10.4 Impact of inflation attack over aggregated result

attack.In SAAQ since MACs sent by each node are verified by its parent node, RMS Error is less when compared to SynDiff. But as the percentage of compromised node increases, the performance deteriorates. SDA-2PV can defend to inflation attack better due to its 2-Phase Verification. In implementation of SDA-2PV, we have assumed that all the nodes send the MAC generated by itself to the base station.

10.5.3 Impact of Deflation Attack

To study the impact of deflation attack, we have launched deflation attack by varying the number of compromised nodes. The results of comparison are shown in Fig. 10.5. All the algorithms can defend better to deflation attack than inflation attack. It can be seen that in both SDA-2PV and SynDiff, the RMS error starts increasing much faster when compared to SAAQ. Both have almost the same RMS error with an increase in the percentage of compromised node because both use adaptive ring topology. SAAQ can withstand better to deflation attack due to the presence of extended adaptive ring's topology.

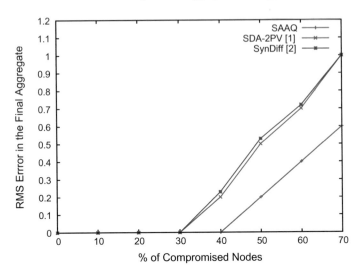

Fig. 10.5   Impact of deflation attack over aggregated result

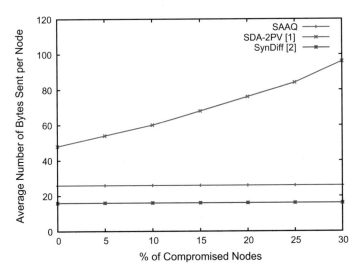

Fig. 10.6   Impact of compromised nodes over number of bytes sent

10.5.4   *Impact of Compromised Nodes on Number of Bytes Sent per Node*

To analyze the impact of compromised nodes on communication overhead, the average number of bytes sent was analyzed per node during each data collection round as shown in Fig. 10.6. The average number of bytes sent per node in SAAQ and Syn-

Diff are constant and does not increase with increase in the number of compromised nodes. In the case of SDA-2PV, for each 1 bit, the node is contributing, Index of the 1 bit and MAC authenticating the 1 bit is transmitted. Hence when inflation attack is launched, the number of 1 bits transmitted increases and hence the number of Indices and MACs resulting in an overall increase in average number of bytes sent per node.

10.6   Summary

The synopsis diffusion framework is robust to communication failure and uses PCSA-based algorithm for generating synopsis [1, 2], while SAAQ uses primitive polynomial modulo 2 for computing synopsis. In order to provide security, each sensor node in SAAQ generates MACs that are verified by all its parents. It provides better security at low communication and computation overhead and hence reduces energy consumption resulting in enhanced lifetime of the WSNs.

References

1. S. Roy, M. Conti, S. Setia, S. Jajodia, Secure data aggregation in wireless sensor networks: filtering out the attackers impact. IEEE Trans. Inf. Forensics Secur. **9**(4), 681–694 (2014)
2. S. Nath, P.B. Gibbons, S. Seshan, Z. Anderson, Synopsis diffusion for robust aggregation in sensor networks, in *Proceedings of International Conference on Embedded Network Sensor Systems (SenSys)* (2004), pp. 250–262
3. J. Considine, F. Li, G. Kollios, J. Byers, Approximate aggregation techniques for sensor databases, in *Proceedings of 20th International Conference on Data Engineering* (2004), pp. 449–460
4. S. Nath, P.B. Gibbons, S. Seshan, Z. Anderson, Synopsis diffusion for robust aggregation in sensor networks. ACM Trans. Sens. Netw. (TOSN) **4**(2), 7 (2008)
5. Y.C. Fan, A.L. Chen, Efficient and robust sensor data aggregation using linear counting sketches, in *Proceedings of IEEE International Symposium on Parallel and Distributed Processing(IPDPS)* (2008), pp. 1–12
6. Y.C. Fan, A.L. Chen, Efficient and robust schemes for sensor data aggregation based on linear counting. IEEE Trans. Parallel Distrib. Syst. **21**(11), 1675–1691 (2010)
7. Y.C. Fan, A.L. Chen, Energy efficient schemes for accuracy-guaranteed sensor data aggregation using scalable counting. IEEE Trans. Knowl. Data Eng. **24**(8), 1463–1477 (2012)
8. S. Tarannum, B. Aravinda, L. Nalini, K.R. Venugopal, L.M. Patnaik, Routing protocol for lifetime maximization of wireless sensor networks, in *Proceedings of International Conference on Advanced Computing and Communications (ADCOM)* (2006), pp. 401–406
9. S. H Manjula, C. Abhilash, K. Shaila, K.R. Venugopal, L.M. Patnaik, Performance of AODV routing protocol using group and entity mobility models in wireless sensor networks, in *Proceedings of the International MultiConference of Engineers and Computer Scientists* (2008), pp. 1212–1217
10. A. Kanavalli, D. Serubiri, P.D. Shenoy, K.R. Venugopal, L.M. Patnaik, A flat routing protocol for sensor networks, in *Proceeding of International Conference on Methods and Models in Computer Science (ICM2CS)* (2009), pp. 1–5

11. U. Prathap, P.D. Shenoy, K.R. Venugopal, L.M. Patnaik, Wireless sensor networks applications and routing protocols: survey and research challenges, in *Proceedings of International Symposium on Cloud and Services Computing (ISCOS)* (2012), pp. 49–56
12. H. Yang, S.H. Wong, S. Lu, L. Zhang, Secure diffusion for wireless sensor networks, in *Proceedings of 3rd International Conference on Broadband Communications, Networks and Systems(BROADNETS)* (2006), pp. 1–10
13. H. Yu, Dos-resilient secure aggregation queries in sensor networks, in *Proceedings of the Twenty-Sixth Annual ACM Symposium on Principles of Distributed Computing* (2007), pp. 394–395
14. M. Garofalakis, J.M. Hellerstein, P. Maniatis, Proof sketches: verifiable in-network aggregation, in *Proceedings of IEEE 23rd International Conference on Data Engineering (ICDE)* (2007), pp. 996–1005
15. S. Nath, H. Yu, H. Chan, Secure outsourced aggregation via one-way chains, in *Proceedings of ACM SIGMOD International Conference on Management of Data, SIGMOD09* (2009), pp. 31–44
16. Y. Yang, X. Wang, S. Zhu, G. Cao, SDAP: a secure hop-by-hop data aggregation protocol for sensor networks. ACM Trans. Inform. Syst. Secur. (TISSEC) **11**(4), 18–43 (2008)
17. S. Roy, S. Setia, S. Jajodia, Attack-resilient hierarchical data aggregation in sensor networks, in *Proceedings of the Fourth ACM Workshop on Security of Ad hoc and Sensor Networks* (2006), pp. 71–82
18. S. Roy, M. Conti, S. Setia, S. Jajodia, Secure data aggregation in wireless sensor networks. IEEE Trans. Inf. Forensics Secur. **7**(3), 1040–1052 (2012)
19. P. Flajolet, G.N. Martin, Probabilistic counting algorithms for data base applications. J. Comput. Syst. Sci. **31**(2), 182–209 (1985)

Further Reading

(1) T. Shiva Prakash, K.B. Raja, K.R. Venugopal, Article: Real-Time Traffic-Differentiated QoS routing for Wireless Sensor Networks. Int. J. Comput. Appl. **87**(10), 6–13

(2) T. Shiva Prakash, K.B. Raja, K.R. Venugopal, Article: Reliable Adaptive Replication Routing for Wireless Sensor Networks. Int. J. Comput. Appl. **114**(17), 1–7, March 2015

(3) M. Kumaraswamy, K. Shaila, V. Tejaswi, K.R. Venugopal, S.S. Iyengar, L.M. Patnaik, QoS driven distributed multi-channel scheduling MAC protocol for multihop WSNs, in *2014 International Conference on Computer and Communication Technology (ICCCT)*. IEEE Explore

(4) T.S. Prakash, G.S. Badrinath, K.R. Venugopal, L.M. Patnaik, Energy Aware Topology management in Ad Hoc Wireless Networks, in *Distributed Computing and Networking* ed. by S. Chaudhuri, S.R. Das, H.S. Paul, S. Tirthapura. ICDCN 2006. Lecture Notes in Computer Science, vol 4308. Springer, Berlin, Heidelberg (2006)

(5) T. Shivaprakash, G.S. Badrinath, S. Chandrakanth, K.R. Venugopal, L.M. Patnaik, Energy Efficient routing in Adhoc Networks, in *Intelligent Sensing and Information Processing (ICISIP), 2006 Fourth International Conference on Intelligent Sensing and Information Processing*. IEEE Explore (2006)

(6) E.G. Prathima, T. ShivPrakash, K.R. Venugopal, S.S. Iyengar , L.M. Patnaik, SDAMQ: Secure Data Aggregation for multiple Queries in Wireless Sensor Networks. Proced. Comput. Sci. **89**, 283–292 (2016).

© Springer Nature Singapore Pte Ltd. 2020
K. R. Venugopal et al., *QoS Routing Algorithms for Wireless Sensor Networks*,
https://doi.org/10.1007/978-981-15-2720-3

Index

© Springer Nature Singapore Pte Ltd. 2020
K. R. Venugopal et al., *QoS Routing Algorithms for Wireless Sensor Networks*,
https://doi.org/10.1007/978-981-15-2720-3